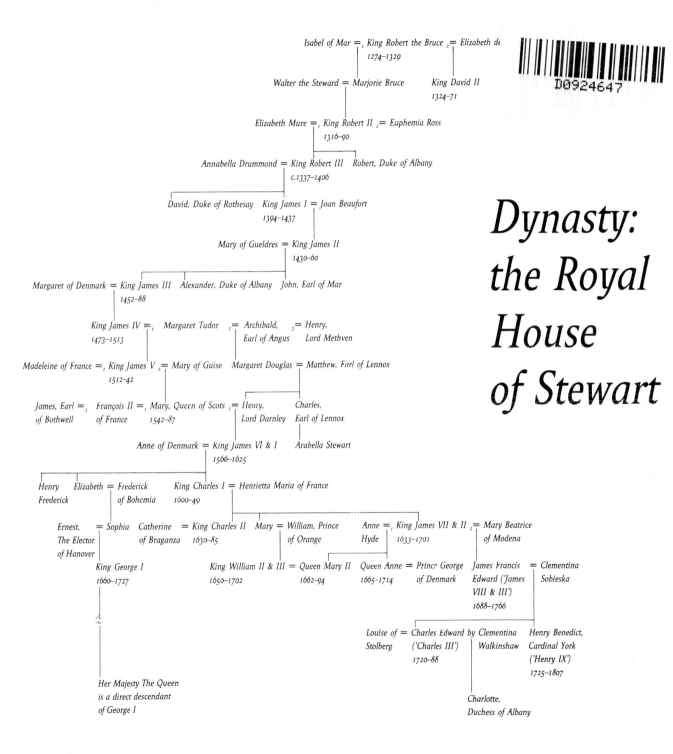

Dynasty: the Royal House of Stewart

Dynasty:
the Royal House of Stewart

by

Duncan Thomson, Rosalind K. Marshall
(Scottish National Portrait Gallery)

David H. Caldwell, Hugh Cheape, George Dalgleish
(National Museums of Scotland)

edited by
Rosalind K. Marshall

National Galleries of Scotland

National Museums of Scotland

Published by the National Galleries of Scotland, The Mound, Edinburgh EH2 2EL and the National Museums of Scotland, Chambers Street, Edinburgh EH1 1JF

Copyright © The Trustees of the National Galleries of Scotland and The Trustees of the National Museums of Scotland, 1990

ISBN 0 903598 02 7

ISBN 0 948636 21 1

Designed by Cinamon and Kitzinger, London, and printed by Alna Press, Broxburn

This publication accompanies the new permanent display Dynasty: the Royal House of Stewart *at the Scottish National Portrait Gallery / Royal Museum of Scotland, 1 Queen Street, Edinburgh EH2 1JD*

The items listed below are in the collections or care of the Scottish National Portrait Gallery.

1, 9, 11, 13, 16, 18, 23, 26, 27, 28, 29, 32, 33, 34, 38, 39, 41, 45, 47, 48, 49, 52, 60, 62, 63, 65, 67, 70, 71, 72, 73, 76, 77, 80, 81, 82, 83, 85, 90, 91, 93, 94, 97, 100, 101, 103, 104, 106, 107, 112, 117, 120, 121, 131, 135, 136, 146, 152, 153, 155, 156, 159, 160.

All of the remainder are in the collections or care of the National Museums of Scotland.

The authors are grateful to Elizabeth Wright and Charles Burnett for additional material for the text.

The medieval kings of Scotland, descendants of Walter the Steward, spelled their surname Stewart. When Mary, Queen of Scots went to France as a child, she was known as Marie Stuart because there is no 'w' in the French alphabet. This spelling became the form favoured by the English branches of the family, but in the interests of consistency and to emphasise their origins, the spelling Stewart has been used throughout this publication.

Cover illustrations: front, Queen Anne by Willem Wissing and Jan van der Vaart (117); back, Stirling Head (24)

Contents

Foreword

In his introduction to the ceremony in the summer of 1889 that marked the opening of the new building in Queen Street in Edinburgh which had been erected to house the Scottish National Portrait Gallery and which was shortly also to become the home of the National Museum of Antiquities, Lord Glencorse, the Lord Justice-General, referred to the bringing together of the two institutions as a 'happy conjunction' that realised the dreams of those eighteenth- and early nineteenth-century antiquaries who had believed that 'National Antiquities and National Portraiture have a natural connection'. These words were echoed by the Secretary for Scotland, Lord Lothian, when he performed the opening ceremony and spoke with evident delight of the 'magnificent collection of antiquities of Scotland' and the prospect that they were soon to be shown under the same roof as the Portrait Gallery's burgeoning collection.

When John Ritchie Findlay, donor of the great new building which was still being completed, came to speak, he initially struck a slightly different note. Telling of his labours over seven years (like Jacob) to create a National Portrait Gallery, he remarked somewhat wryly on the Leah that had been thrust upon him and the fact that he had 'had to provide house-room for two institutions instead of one!' But his remarks were clearly good-humoured and he went on to refer to the association as 'a peculiarly felicitous conjunction' and his belief that the 'two collections would be mutually illustrative of our national history'.

And indeed they have been, for virtually one hundred years, although Findlay's slightly ambivalent view was perhaps reflected in the fact that the displays in the two halves of the building remained separate. Nevertheless, there has always been happy co-operation in terms of mutual lending, joint temporary exhibitions and sharing of expertise between the two institutions.

Time has inevitably brought change, both constitutionally and to ideas of historical display. The Portrait Gallery is now part of that wider entity, the National Galleries of Scotland, and the former Museum of Antiquities has been absorbed into the new National Museums of Scotland. Yet, for a little longer, both collections will remain together in Findlay's building.

While that continues to be the case, the opportunity has at long last been taken to shape at least parts of the two collections to the needs of a public (even the local one) that has always been a little puzzled by the invisible, but real, barrier between them. This major step has led to a fully integrated display on the ground floor of the building which tells the story of the Stewart dynasty from the fourteenth century to the end of the period of the Jacobite claimants to the British throne. We are convinced that this new initiative will break down old barriers and that both the new display and this publication which accompanies it will help towards a fuller understanding of an important area of Scottish history.

Robert Anderson
Director
National Museums of Scotland

Timothy Clifford
Director
National Galleries of Scotland

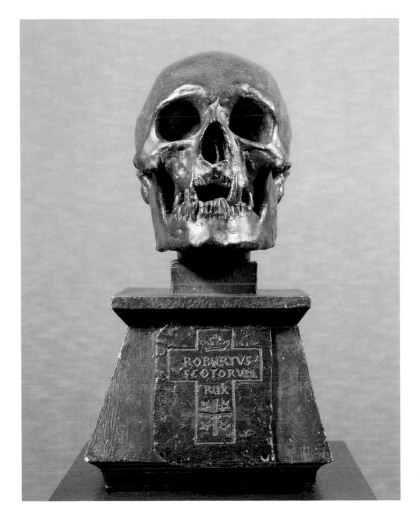

1. *Skull of King Robert the Bruce*
plaster cast
by William Scoular

Introduction

FOR more than three hundred years the Stewart kings ruled Scotland. While York and Lancaster vied for supremacy in England only to be supplanted by the Tudors, while Bourbon replaced Valois in France, the Scottish crown passed directly from father (or mother) to child or brother for twelve generations. This continuity was all the more surprising because the Stewarts' lives were so dogged by personal tragedy. Murder, accident and unexpected illness carried off first one and then another in the prime of life, leaving their turbulent nobility to contend for control of the latest child king.

3. *The Bute Mazer*
about 1315 and later
detail of silver-gilt central boss
Lent by the Marquis of Bute

2. *Fragments of King Robert the Bruce's tomb*
about 1329

Scotland's great hero, King Robert the Bruce, ancestor of the Stewarts, was the man who had led his army to victory against the English at Bannockburn when Edward II threatened the independence of the Scottish nation. King Robert's tomb was uncovered in the Abbey Church of Dunfermline early in 1818, when the foundations of a new church were being dug. It lay on the precise centre line of the old church. The principal contents of the stone-lined chamber beneath the floor were the almost totally decayed remains of a wooden coffin, and a skeleton of a man about six feet in height, wrapped in two thin sheets of lead and covered with a cloth of gold. The remains were identified as those of King Robert. They were

examined carefully on 5 November 1819 and a plaster cast of the skull (fig. 1) was made by the sculptor William Scoular. The tomb was then sealed up.

King Robert the Bruce's grave was situated in front of the high altar of the Abbey Church, and over it had been erected an alabaster monument, fragments of which were recovered (fig. 2). The monument was commissioned while the King was still alive and had been carved in Paris by Thomas of Chartres.

In the decoration on a communal drinking cup, the Bute Mazer, Robert the Bruce is represented by a lion. Between the lion's paws is the shield of Walter the Steward, Bruce's son-in-law, and surrounding it are the shields of some of his chief supporters. These include the arms of the Fitzgilbert who was keeper of the Steward's Castle of Rothesay, and it has been suggested that he commissioned this mazer to celebrate a gathering there of these nobles.

The Mazer has a silver rim which bears the name of Ninian Bannatyne of Kames, a sixteenth-century laird on the Island of Bute, but the silver-gilt boss in the centre of the bowl (fig. 3) and possibly the wooden bowl itself are of earlier date.

4. The Kames Brooch
about 1300

Somehow or other, the Stewarts survived: 'a famous dynasty', as one eminent historian has put it, 'which was to produce so many men of remarkable ability and so many men and women with fascinating and commanding personalities'. Their story contains all the elements of high drama, and if some of the legends about 'James of the Fiery Face' and 'the Guid Man o' Ballengeich' owe more to imagination than to hard, historical fact, then the Stewarts themselves bear part of the responsibility. They created their own myth that they were descendants of Scota, daughter of the Egyptian Pharaoh.

Whatever their true origins, they first came to Scotland from France, where they were stewards of the Archbishops of Dol, near Mont-St-Michel. After a sojourn in England, they took up office as stewards of the Scottish kings and by the late twelfth century they were hereditary High Stewards of Scotland. The most significant moment in their history came in 1314, however, when Walter, the sixth High Steward, married Marjorie, the daughter of King Robert the Bruce. Two years later, in the final stages of pregnancy, she died after a fall from her horse, but her son was born alive. Fifty-five years on, he would become Robert II, King of Scots, founder of his dynasty.

5. *Effigy of Sir James Douglas*
about 1330
cast

One of the ladies at Bruce's court may have owned the gold ring brooch (**fig. 4**) which has long been associated with the Bute Mazer and may have graced the same events. It is cast with a chain of six wyverns (heraldic beasts with dragons' heads, winged bodies and serpents' tails), each gripping the one in front with left fore-paw and teeth, and curling its tail around the neck of the one behind. The back is engraved with a talismanic inscription incorporating the name of Jesus, two of the Magi and one of the Fates.

Sir James Douglas, 'Good Sir James', was a patriot and companion of Robert the Bruce, and one of the most able soldiers of his time. He died fighting in Spain in 1330, on his way to the Holy Land with Bruce's heart. His effigy, a cast of which is reproduced (**fig. 5**), shows him ready for battle, clad in a mail hauberk, chausses (leggings) and coif (helmet). Over the hauberk he wears a long flowing surcoat and he is armed with a sword and shield.

6. Groat of King Robert II

Robert II
1316–90

NO portrait of Robert II exists, although a description from 1385 unkindly says that he had 'eyes the colour of sandalwood, which clearly showed he was no valiant man but one who would rather remain at home than march the field'. He was seventy by then, and if he longed for peace it was hardly surprising.

When Robert the Bruce died in 1329 his five-year-old son became King David II. The English seized the opportunity to support the cause of a rival claimant to the throne, Edward Balliol, and Robert Stewart, the new king's nephew, grew up against a background of war and the rumour of war. Few details of his early days are known, merely the bare genealogical facts.

At seventeen, Robert was leading the Scots into battle and defeat by the English at Halidon Hill. Soon afterwards, the boy King was sent to France for safety and by the time Robert was in his mid-twenties he was ruling as regent, for he was David's nearest heir. After seven years, the King came back, but in 1346 he was captured fighting the English at Neville's Cross. Robert, who had been with him, escaped, and his enemies said that he had deliberately abandoned David to his fate.

Regent once more, he ruled the country for eleven years until the King was released. Relinquishing power, he could console himself with the thought that while David remained childless, his own two marriages had brought him thirteen children in addition to his eight illegitimate sons. In the event, he himself inherited the throne on his uncle's sudden death in 1371. An old man by medieval standards, he struggled to prevent his pugnacious subjects from renewing the war with England while his ambitious sons vied with each other for power. In the last decade of his life the eldest, John, and the second son, Robert, helped him to rule. He died in 1390 after an undistinguished reign.

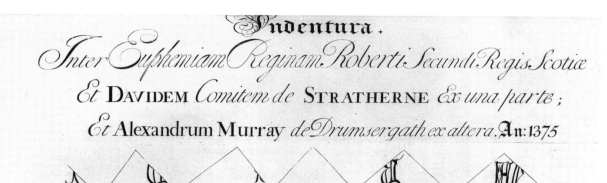

Indentura.

Inter Euphemiam Reginam Roberti Secundi Regis Scotiae
Et DAVIDEM Comitem de STRATHERNE Ex una parte;
Et Alexandrum Murray de Drumsergath ex altera. An: 1375

Coins are an important symbol of nationhood and a means of dynastic advertisement. The coin illustrated (**fig. 6**) bears a picture of the King, but it is not a real portrait, simply a stylised image similar to those on coins produced elsewhere in Europe.

The sons of Euphemia Ross, second Queen of Robert II, always claimed that their father's first marriage, to Elizabeth Mure, was invalid and that the eldest of them, David, was the true heir to the throne. A document of 1375 (**fig. 7**) refers to the lands and titles of Euphemia's sons which reinforced their threat to the succession.

Diplomata Scotiae, in which this document is reproduced, is a collection of facsimiles of early documents, coins and seals, prepared by James Anderson, a seventeenth-century Edinburgh lawyer, to disprove the contention of English historians and pamphleteers that Edward I of England's claims to the Scottish crown were legitimate and that certain charters made a mockery of Scottish independence. Anderson showed that these charters were medieval forgeries and at the same time he created an awareness of the importance of original documents to historical study.

7. *Indenture of 1375*
by Euphemia Ross
from Diplomata Scotiae,
1739

8. *Groat of King Robert III*

Robert III
about 1337–1406

ROBERT II's later years had been disturbed by the quarrelling of his sons. The eldest, John, was gentle and unaggressive but Alexander, the youngest, was known as 'The Wolf of Badenoch' after he burned Elgin Cathedral, and Robert, the second son, was continually vying with John for supremacy. An unfortunate accident put an abrupt end to John's period of helping his father to govern Scotland: a kick by a horse permanently affected his health and Robert, later Duke of Albany, seized the opportunity of supplanting him as the King's chief confidant.

Albany clearly hoped to succeed to the throne, but on his father's death the crown passed to his brother John. Since the name was regarded as being an unlucky one for kings, he chose to be known as Robert III. Already fifty-three, he was dominated by Albany, who was determined to cling to power. When Robert did attempt to govern by himself in 1393 chaos ensued. 'He who was strong oppressed the weak and the whole kingdom was one den of thieves', one chronicler reported. Robert was painfully aware of his own deficiencies. 'Bury me in a midden', he said once, 'and write, "Here lies the worst of kings and the most wretched of men"'.

In 1395, parliament condemned his misgovernment and appointed his elder son David, Duke of Rothesay, to rule for him. Albany remained the leading counsellor, however, and before long he had David arrested and imprisoned. The young man's mysterious death at Falkland Palace in 1402 gave rise to rumours that Albany had starved him to death. In the aftermath of the alleged murder, Robert III seems to have feared for his own life. In 1406 he retired to the greater safety of Rothesay Castle, arranging for his remaining son, James, to go to France. On the way south, the Prince was captured by English pirates off Flamborough Head. When the news was brought to Robert it was the final blow. He died shortly afterwards.

IACOBVS I L·GRATIA·
REX· SCOTORVM·

9. James I
oil on panel
by an unknown artist

James I
1394–1437

AFTER his capture, James was taken to the English King, Henry IV, who commented sardonically that there had been no need for him to go as far as France to learn French: he himself could act as the Prince's teacher. In fact, he did allow James to live at court and he made sure that he was educated in a suitable manner. By the time he was eighteen, the young King of Scots was mature, energetic and accomplished. He was also growing increasingly impatient that Albany, ruling Scotland in his place, was making no attempt to negotiate his release.

Not until he was in his late twenties did he gain his freedom. One day, as he looked from his window, he saw a beautiful young woman strolling in the gardens beneath and immediately fell in love with her. She was Lady Joan Beaufort, a close relative of the English King. She was equally attracted to James, and it was probably through her influence that the English sealed the Treaty of London in December 1423, agreeing to release their royal prisoner in return for a ransom of £40,000.

James and Joan were married a few weeks later, and he took her back to Scotland the following April. Their domestic life was happy. She bore him twin sons and six daughters, and he painted, drew, wrote poetry, loved music and was a fine athlete. His overwhelming ambition, however, was to put his country in order after his long absence, making 'the key keep the castle and the bracken bush the cow'. Albany was dead by now, but the nobility had gained far too much power. James set about seizing the lands of his most troublesome lords. He taxed them heavily, dealt severely with the Highland chiefs and tried to bring peace and justice to all sections of society. In so doing he made many enemies, and on 20 February 1437 a group of conspirators forced their way into the Charterhouse in Perth where he was staying, flung aside Catherine Douglas who tried to bar the door against them with her arm, seriously wounded the Queen and stabbed the King to death.

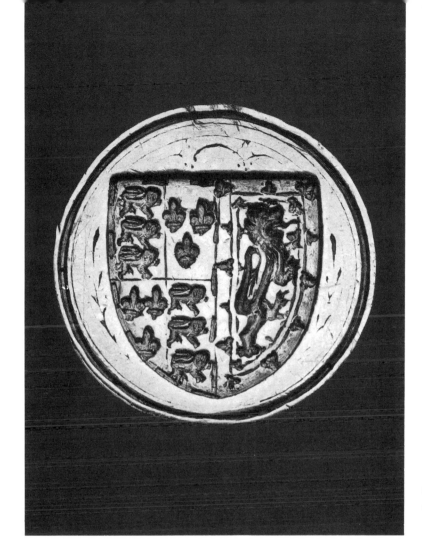

10. *Gold seal of Queen Joan Beaufort* about 1425

Series of portraits of monarchs or 'famous men' were common in Europe from the Renaissance onwards. They represented a reverence for the past and the idea of continuity, so the artists were not particularly concerned with individual likenesses. If, however, evidence of the subject's true appearance existed, it was likely to be used. The portrait of James I (**fig. 9**) is one of a small group of panel portraits of James I to James V, by unknown artists, probably painted in the late sixteenth century. All five of these portraits appear to be based on earlier likenesses. That of James III is certainly derived from the portrait on the three-quarter face groat of about 1485 (**fig. 14**).

Images of this sort are often associated with the triumphal arches erected in cities for the ceremonial entry of a particular monarch. In this case it is tempting to associate the five portraits with the entry of James VI into Edinburgh in 1579, when an arch at the Saltmarket Cross bore a genealogy of the Kings of Scotland. It is highly probable that the genealogy was decorated with actual portraits.

The gold signet (**fig. 10**) of James I's Queen has two hinged flaps on its back for grasping when in use. The design consists of the impaled arms of Scotland, and France and England quarterly, surrounded by foliage.

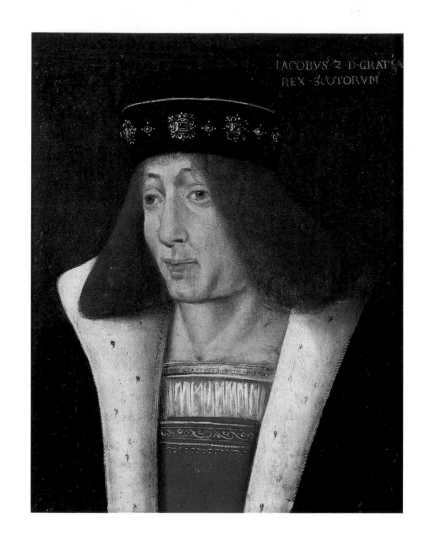

IACOBVS 2 D·GRATIA REX ·SCOTORVM

11. *James II*
oil on panel
by an unknown artist
(see fig. 9)

James II
1430–60

WITH the death of James I, Queen Joan began to rule as regent on behalf of their six-year-old son, 'James of the Fiery Face', so called because of a disfiguring birthmark. When Joan remarried she was replaced by Archibald, 5th Earl of Douglas, one of Scotland's most powerful magnates. He died when James was eight, whereupon two ambitious men, Sir William Crichton and Sir Alexander Livingston, took charge. Fearing that they would be supplanted by Douglas's son when he grew to manhood, they invited the young Earl and his brother to visit the King in Edinburgh Castle. The boys talked happily together as they sat down to dine, but when they saw a servant carry in a black bull's head, the sign of

12. *Finds from Threave Castle*

The King's campaign against the Douglas family culminated in the siege of the Douglas stronghold of Threave, in Kirkcudbright, in 1456. Excavations there have recovered military equipment (**fig. 12**) including arrowheads, gunstones and a piece of corroded mail. The castle was eventually taken, but not without payments being made by James to some of the garrison.

death, they leaped up in terror. Before James's horrified gaze, his friends were dragged out and put to death.

As the years went by, Livingston gradually managed to oust Crichton, putting his own relatives in all the important offices of state. Meanwhile James was growing to adulthood and when he was eighteen he married. His bride was a pious, cultivated Burgundian lady, Mary, daughter of the Duke of Gueldres, and it was perhaps with her encouragement that he seized power and began to rule for himself.

The Livingstons were removed, but the Douglas family remained a tremendous threat. They had earned considerable military prestige as well as possessing vast estates, and when the King heard that the 8th Earl was making a treaty with the Earl of Crawford and the Lord of the Isles he was immediately suspicious that they were plotting against him. He summoned Douglas to Stirling Castle, guaranteeing him a safe-conduct, but they quarrelled violently and James stabbed him to death. He then greatly increased the power of the crown by seizing large tracts of territory, and was so successful in maintaining law and order that in 1458 parliament passed a special vote of thanks.

Two years later he decided to besiege Roxburgh Castle, held by the English for more than a century. As he stood close to one of his cannon directing operations it exploded, killing him instantly.

13. *James III*
oil on panel
by an unknown artist
(see fig. 9)

James III
1452–88

WITH the unexpected death of James II, Scotland was once more plunged into a royal minority, for his eldest son was only eight. The boy's mother resolutely began to rule on his behalf, advised by Bishop James Kennedy, but when these two wise Regents died, the Boyd family seized power. Their period of dominance lasted until 1469, when James III married the saintly Princess Margaret of Denmark and, at seventeen, began ruling for himself.

In character James is something of an enigma. Condemned by contemporaries and censured by later historians for being weak and grasping, he nonetheless seems to have possessed all the Stewarts' energy as well as his mother's piety and her devotion to the arts. He loved architecture, music and fine books, and he preferred the company of scholars, artists, architects and musicians to that of his increasingly resentful nobles.

His own brothers, John, Earl of Mar, and Alexander, Duke of Albany, regarded him with jealousy verging on hatred. John was to die in

14. *Groat of King James III* about 1485

mysterious circumstances and Alexander would invade Scotland twice at the head of an English army. On the first occasion, the rebellious Scottish nobles seized the opportunity of demanding that the King dismiss his low-born favourites and, when he refused, they hanged them from Lauder Bridge.

After his Queen's death in 1486, James lived in seclusion in Stirling Castle amidst growing rumours of his cupidity and his unsuitable friendship with England. Finally, the nobles seized his eldest son and confronted the King on the battlefield of Sauchieburn. James was defeated. As he left the field, his horse shied and threw him. He was carried into a nearby cottage, where a woman asked him who he was. 'I was your King this day at morn', he answered grimly, and called for a priest. At that, a mysterious stranger forced his way in and stood over him. 'I will shrive thee!' the man exclaimed and, drawing out a knife, he stabbed James III to death.

15. *Lintel with royal arms*
about 1480
from a house in Leith

James is the first Scottish king whose features are reliably known to us, from his coinage and from the Trinity Altarpiece. A groat of about 1485 (**fig. 14**) is of unique importance because the image of the King is a true portrait. It is related in some respects to the portrait of James in the altarpiece painted a few years earlier by the Flemish artist Hugo van der Goes for the Church of the Holy Trinity in Edinburgh. However, the spatial qualities of the three-quarter view of the face, and its liveliness, relate it to Italian Renaissance art. Even in that context it would stand out as something unusual. It is a puzzling landmark in the history of Scottish portraits.

Heraldic devices were of great symbolic importance. In 1471 the Scottish parliament passed an act doing away with the double tressure around the lion on the royal arms. At that time James III was contemplating a visit to the French court and perhaps parliament did not want this decoration with its fleurs-de-lys to indicate that Scotland was in any way under French domination. In the event, to avoid confusion with other arms, only the top part of the tressure was removed, as on a stone which may have come from the King's Wark, a royal property in Leith used as a warehouse (**fig. 15**).

16. *James IV*
oil on panel
by an unknown artist
(see fig. 9)

James IV
1473–1513

JAMES IV was fifteen when his father's enemies forced him to ride with them to Sauchieburn, and for the rest of his life he wore an iron belt round his waist as a penance. He was able to start ruling for himself at once, for as the great scholar Erasmus observed, 'He had wonderful powers of mind, an astonishing knowledge of everything, an unconquerable magnanimity and the most abundant generosity.' A Spanish visitor added this description: King James was, he wrote, 'of noble stature, neither tall nor short, and as handsome in complexion and shape as a man can be'. He spoke Latin (the international language of the time), French, German, Flemish, Italian, Spanish and some Gaelic, and he took an active interest in literature, science and the law as well as trying his hand at dentistry and minor surgery.

The Royal College of Surgeons of Edinburgh, St Leonard's College, St Andrews, and King's College, Aberdeen, were founded during his reign and in 1508 the printing press came to Scotland under his patronage. He undertook building work at his castles of Edinburgh and Stirling as well as at Linlithgow Palace. Determined to establish a strong central government, he suppressed the troublesome Lordship of the Isles, annexing its vast territories to the crown.

Eager to build up Scotland's defences, he created a strong navy led by his ship the *Great Michael*, but he was even more anxious for peace with England and after the tragic death of his mistress Margaret Drummond, who was poisoned along with her sisters, he accepted Henry VII's offer of his daughter Margaret Tudor as a bride. 'The Marriage of the Thistle and the Rose' took place in 1503. Although this alliance was to be of great importance in the long-term, it did not immediately bring about the expected improvement in Anglo-Scottish relations and when the English invaded France, James felt compelled to come to the assistance of his old ally. He led his army south in 1513, to die at the head of his men in the disastrous battle of Flodden.

17. *The Great Seal of James IV*
cast

The Great Seal (**fig. 17**) was used to authenticate all important documents issued in the King's name. A silver matrix was used to impress the seal in wax which was then attached to the foot of the document. This seal of James IV is essentially the same design used by all the Stewart kings from James I to James V. On one side the King is shown enthroned with sceptre in hand, ready to dispense justice. On the other he is in armour on horseback, ready to do battle.

18. *James V*
oil on panel
by an unknown artist
(see fig. 9)

James V
1512–42

JAMES V was a year old when his father was killed at Flodden and the Scots were reluctant to accept his English mother as Regent. When she remarried the following year, parliament chose the heir apparent to the throne, James IV's half-French cousin, the Duke of Albany, to take her place and he ruled conscientiously for the next ten years. Meanwhile, Margaret's tempestuous private life complicated her son's childhood. Tiring of her new husband, the Earl of Angus, she decided to divorce him,

19. *John Stewart, Duke of Albany* gold medal, 1524

20. *Groat of King James V*

The Duke of Albany finally returned to France after his period of regency in 1542, the year a medal (**fig. 19**) was struck showing on its obverse the conjoined arms of the Duke and of his wife, who died that same year. The reverse has the Holy Dove perched on the Duke's arms. It is thought the medal was made of Scottish gold.

The portraits on some of James's coinage look quite lifelike (**fig. 20**), but this bust had been copied from the early coins of his uncle, King Henry VIII of England.

James V undertook important building work at Linlithgow Palace, a favourite royal residence. Although no contemporary view exists, a late seventeenth-century engraving by John Slezer (**fig. 21**) shows the ranges of domestic buildings at the palace with the significant Renaissance detailing created by James and his grandson, James VI. At the same time it provides an interesting glimpse of the surrounding countryside with its open fields and meandering roads.

Slezer was a Dutch artilleryman who settled in Scotland and undertook a project to record all the royal residences, the abbeys, burghs and noble houses in the kingdom.

Prospectus Regis Palatis LIMNUCHENSIS. *The Prospect of Their Maj.ties Palace of* LINLITHGOW.

10.

21. *Linlithgow Palace* from *Theatrum Scotiae*, 1693, a collection of engravings by John Slezer

whereupon he kidnapped the fourteen-year-old King. Although he showered James with gifts and introduced him to a round of highly unsuitable pleasures, James loathed the Earl and two years later managed to escape.

A highly-strung, intelligent man, given to bouts of black depression alternating with feverish pursuit of excitement, James had fathered at least nine illegitimate children by the time he decided to marry in 1537. Eager to strengthen the Auld Alliance, he chose the French Princess Madeleine as his bride, but her delicate health could not survive the rigours of the Scottish climate and she died two months after her arrival. A year later James married Mary of Guise, an aristocratic French widow, handsome, six feet tall and already the mother of two sons. She and James had two boys of their own, but they died tragically in infancy, within hours of each other. The King was inconsolable. Convinced that they had been poisoned, he was suspicious of everyone around him, and indeed many of his lords were secretly accepting pensions from the English. Determined to do battle with Henry VIII's forces, he led his army south in 1542 to total defeat at Solway Moss.

The King thereupon suffered a complete nervous collapse. He took to his bed in Falkland Palace and when a messenger came to tell him that his wife had given birth to a daughter instead of the hoped-for son, he believed that the end of his dynasty was at hand. 'It cam' wi' a lass and it will gang wi' a lass', he said, remembering how the crown had come to the Stewarts through Marjorie Bruce. Six days later he was dead.

22. *Armorial of Sir David Lyndsay of the Mount, 1542*
facsimile edition of 1822
engraved by W. H. Lizars and hand coloured on vellum

Sir David Lyndsay was Lyon King of Arms (the chief herald of Scotland) to King James V and drew up an heraldic record book (**fig. 22**). It begins with the royal arms of Scotland, includes the arms of successive Scottish kings and records the arms of all the Scottish peers.

Lyndsay was also one of the greatest writers in the Scots vernacular tradition. His most famous work, *Ane Satyre of the Thrie Estaitis*, was a biting attack on ecclesiastical excess and on James V's own immorality in the period before he married.

Mary of Guise (**fig. 23**) married James V in a proxy ceremony and

23. *Mary of Guise (1515–60)* oil on panel attributed to Corneille de Lyon

came to Scotland the following year. Her pursuit of power after James's death culminated in her becoming regent for their daughter, Mary, Queen of Scots, in 1554. Her alliance with France against the Protestant Reformers led to civil war and she died under siege in Edinburgh Castle.

This small portrait, of exceptional quality, must have been painted either before her years in Scotland or during her lengthy return visit to France in 1550. The size of the painting and its leaf-green background are characteristic of Corneille de Lyon's portraits, although the face lacks his usual shadows. The identity is confirmed by a drawing of the Queen in the British Museum.

James V visited the court of his ally, François I, and married two successive French wives, so it is not surprising that the Scottish court rapidly adopted the new Renaissance style in vogue in France. This is seen most impressively in the royal palaces at Falkland and Stirling. The Stirling Heads are from the ceiling of the King's Presence Chamber in the palace in Stirling Castle. Over thirty of these carved oak medallions survive, some with figures from history and mythology, others apparently with representations of contemporaries.

The two heads illustrated (**fig. 24**) are thought to represent Margaret Tudor and her son James V. (A third head depicts a dancing child, a favourite image in Renaissance art.) The heads are of a high

24. *The Stirling Heads*
carved oak medallions
about 1540

25. *Wooden panel with royal arms*
about 1540–70
from Linlithgow Palace

standard of design and craftsmanship and are probably the work of French carvers.

A wooden panel (**fig. 25**) from Linlithgow Palace, birthplace of Mary, Queen of Scots, was perhaps intended to show the arms of Mary below those of her father, James V. The arms have unicorn supporters and a facing helm; below is a tressured shield with its centre cut away: that has unicorn supporters, but a profile helm.

26. *Mary, Queen of Scots*
oil on canvas
perhaps by Rowland Lockey

Mary, Queen of Scots
1542–87

ATATIS SVÆ 32

HADDINGTVN TOVN

ANO DOMINNI 1547

Taken and defended agaynst tow belegen of ye Scots alsere
of ye Frutche bie the valure of the Englishe men.
this Knight being theyre Centeynt.

27. *Sir James Wilsford*
(1515–50)
oil on panel, dated 1547
by an unknown artist

WHEN Mary became Queen at six days old, the Scottish nobility decided to make peace with England by marrying her to Henry VIII's son, the future Edward VI. No sooner was the treaty arranged than they began to regret it, and to Henry's fury they broke off the match. In spite of his army's devastating raids, 'The Rough Wooing', the Scots betrothed their Queen to the French King's heir and sent her to be brought up in France.

Mary married the Dauphin François in 1558. Tall, graceful and quick-witted, she was the centre of attention at her husband's court until his premature death. Seeing no place for herself in a country ruled by her hostile mother-in-law, in 1561 she returned to Scotland, now an officially Protestant country.

Advised by her half-brother James, Earl of Moray and the subtle William Maitland of Lethington, Mary ruled with moderation. Her principal ambitions were to marry a Roman Catholic monarch, and to have her claim to the English throne recognised by Queen Elizabeth. Balked in her attempts to find the husband she wanted, she chose Henry, Lord Darnley, who had Tudor blood in his veins.

Darnley was immature and easily inveigled by Mary's enemies into plotting against her. He was one of those who burst into her supper chamber and murdered her secretary, David Riccio. The birth of their son James did nothing to improve matters between Mary and Darnley, and when he was murdered at Kirk o' Field, many people were ready to accuse her of complicity in the crime. Her subsequent marriage to the Earl of

28. *François II (1544–60)*
enamel
attributed to Leonard Limosin I

Sir James Wilsford (**fig. 27**) was a commander in the English army which invaded Scotland during 'The Rough Wooing' in 1547. He took part in the capture of Haddington and became its governor, the role in which he is depicted. The view of Haddington in the distance is likely to be a conventional one rather than an exact record, although the hill could be intended to represent Berwick Law. This portrait has the qualities of an icon, but with a surprising touch of realism in the great scar shown on his forehead, the wound from which he probably died three years later.

The Dauphin, later François II, of France married Mary in April

29. *George Seton,*
5th Lord Seton
(about 1533–85)
oil on panel,
dated 157[?]
attributed to
Adrian Vanson

1558. Likely to have been made shortly before the wedding, this painted enamel portrait (**fig. 28**) is very close in almost every respect to a drawing by François Clouet. Limosin, who worked at Limoges in an Italian mannerist style, produced portraits of this sort for Henri II which were often intended to be inset in richly carved and decorated furniture.

George Seton (**fig. 29**) was Master of the Household to Mary, Queen of Scots, and he is shown in his thistle-embroidered livery carrying his staff of office decorated with her cipher. He was dressed thus when he attended her wedding to the Dauphin François in Notre

Dame Cathedral in 1558, but this picture is retrospective, for it was not painted until the late 1570s. It probably derives from a portrait of 1572 by the French painter François Pourbus showing Seton with his family. There is a strong sense in which the painting refers to former glory, with the main inscription reading, in translation: 'In adversity, unyielding, in prosperity, generous'. The pillar itself is a conventional symbol of fortitude, appropriate to 'the Loyal Seton's' lifelong support of his Queen.

In January 1563 Michael Gilbert, an Edinburgh goldsmith, was called before the Lords of Secret Council and required to deliver the

Bothwell, generally recognised as the principal murderer, brought inevitable ruin.

The Protestant Lords rose against her, she surrendered at Carberry Hill, was imprisoned in Lochleven Castle and forced to abdicate in favour of her infant son. She escaped in 1568, only to be defeated at the battle of Langside and fled to England, hoping that Queen Elizabeth would assist her. Instead, she spent her last nineteen years in captivity. She was executed at Fotheringhay on 8 February 1587 for conspiring against the English Queen.

30. The initials of George, Lord Seton and his wife Elizabeth gold medal, 1562

31. Gold ducat of François and Mary 1558

punches for his medal of George Seton and his wife (**fig. 30**) to the Warden of the Mint. Perhaps the Lords feared the medals were too like coins. On the obverse are the conjoined initials of husband and wife and on the reverse a design of a thistle in a trefoil.

Soon after Mary's first marriage a gold ducat coin (**fig. 31**) was issued which provides the earliest Scottish example of two busts appearing on one coin. The design was inspired by the shillings of Queen Mary Tudor of England with her husband Philip II of Spain. The reverse has a cross design incorporating dolphins for François and Lorraine crosses for Mary's mother.

The bronze bust (**fig. 32**) shows the 17- or 18-year-old Queen wearing the closed Imperial French crown made of linked fleurs-de-lys. Mary reigned as Queen of France between July 1559 and December 1560. Although there is a strong resemblance between this bust and other contemporary portraits of her, the artist was working in the rather artificial style that characterised the northern variety of Italian mannerism fashionable at the French court. This is the finest of three known casts, the modelling both sharp and refined. The other two are in the Louvre, Paris, and the Victoria and Albert Museum, London.

33. *Mary, Queen of Scots*
oil on panel
by an unknown artist

32. *Mary, Queen of Scots*
bronze bust
by Ponce Jacquio

Mary's father-in-law, Henri II of France, died in July 1559 after being wounded while jousting. Her husband, François II, died in December 1560 of an ear infection. As early as August 1560 she had discussed with the English ambassador his desire to have her 'picture when I wore the *deuil*' and it is therefore probably for her father-in-law that she is wearing the white mourning (*deuil blanc*) in which she is shown (**fig. 33**). The portrait in question was intended for Queen Elizabeth.

Several versions exist, all derived from a chalk drawing by the court painter François Clouet.

34. *Henry Stewart, Lord Darnley (1545–67)*
oil on panel, dated 1555
by Hans Eworth

35. *The Queen Mary Harp*

While Mary was living in France, her future husband, Lord Darnley, was growing up in England. When he was nine his proud parents commissioned a portrait showing the boy's undoubted physical attractiveness and also emphasising his dynastic significance (**fig. 34**). His mother, the Countess of Lennox, was the niece of Henry VIII and through her he had a claim to the English throne, while his father, the Earl, was a descendant of James II of Scotland. Ten years after this portrait was painted Darnley travelled to Scotland and married Mary, Queen of Scots. The painting was given by the Duke of Lennox to Darnley's grandson, Charles I, in 1639.

The short reign of Queen Mary, beginning in 1562, saw some revival of music-making at court, and the Queen herself was an inspiration to musicians and poets. A clarsach or Highland harp (**fig. 35**) is said to have been given by Mary, Queen of Scots, to Beatrix Gardyn of Banchory when the Queen was on a hunting expedition in the Highlands in 1563. It is constructed in three parts, the soundbox or *com*, the forepillar or *lamh-chrann*, and the harmonic curve or *corr* joining the two sections at the top. The surfaces are decorated with geometrical patterns, scroll work of leaves and foliage, and fabulous beasts. The instrument is made from a hardwood, probably hornbeam, and the soundbox has been hollowed out of the solid.

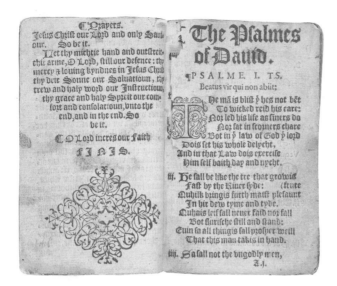

36. *The Book of Common Order and Psalter*
about 1576

37. *The Queen Mary Cup*
second half of the sixteenth century
by Christopher Lindenberger, Nürnberg
Lent by the Kirk Session of St John's Kirk, Perth

The Reformation of 1560 brought a radical reorganisation of the church in Scotland. The provision of a liturgy in the vernacular instead of in Latin meant that congregations could now take part in the services of the Reformed Church. Familiarly known as 'the Psalmbook', the official name of the service book ordered by the General Assembly was 'The Book of Common Order'.

A possibly unique copy has survived of the Prayer Book and Psalms printed in Scots in Edinburgh (**fig. 36**). Lacking a title page, it is printed mainly in black-letter type with roman headings, probably by Robert Lekprevick, who was working at the Netherbow in Edinburgh in the 1560s. He later became the King's printer.

Traditionally said to have been given by Mary, Queen of Scots to St John's Kirk in Perth, the cup shown (**fig. 37**) would originally have been a secular drinking vessel. It was certainly in the kirk's possession by 1632. The lid was remodelled about 1640 by Robert Gairdyne, a Dundee goldsmith, who probably also engraved the words 'for the Kirk of Perth' on the body.

A later portrait of Lord Darnley (**fig. 38**) appears to have been painted shortly before his journey to Scotland. However, the cartouche in the top corner must have been added rather later, for it refers quite precisely to the date of his death.

38. *Henry Stewart, Lord Darnley (1545–67)*
oil on panel
by an unknown artist

39. *Medal commemorating the marriage of Mary and Darnley*
silver, 1565

The artist is likely to have been someone working in Hans Eworth's workshop. Like the portrait of Darnley as a young boy, this picture also once belonged to Charles I. His cipher, a crowned 'CR', is branded on the back of the panel on which it is painted.

Just before their wedding, Mary bestowed on Darnley the title 'King of Scots' without the sanction of parliament. This title is used on a medal (**fig. 39**) which has on its obverse facing busts of the married couple, and on its reverse the royal arms.

The finely decorated oak cabinet illustrated (**fig. 40**) is in the Renaissance style. The doors are divided into sixteen 'romayne' panels, each containing a representation of a human head, eight of them men and eight women, projecting boldly from the panel surface. The heads are enclosed in circular wreaths surrounded by foliage. The central column terminates in a carving of the Virgin and Child.

The cabinet was imported from France and there would not have been many pieces of furniture of this quality in sixteenth-century Scotland. It was bequeathed by a descendant of a family of East Lothian lairds who believed it had belonged to Mary, Queen of Scots and indeed, it may have come from one of the royal palaces.

40. *Oak cabinet*
mid sixteenth century

Mary married her third husband, the Earl of Bothwell, in 1567. The wedding of Bothwell to his first wife in February 1566 had presumably been the occasion for the pair of tiny portraits on copper (**fig. 41**). They are strongly Franco-Netherlandish in style, perhaps by one of the Pourbus family, and it is difficult to understand the circumstances in which they were painted. Bothwell travelled frequently in Northern Europe, but not, apparently, in 1566, and there are no records of his wife ever having been there. The authenticity of the likenesses, however, is strongly supported by the close similarity of the Countess's portrait to one at Dunrobin Castle of her in old age.

After her brief marriage to Bothwell was ended so that he could marry Mary, Queen of Scots, Jean went on to marry the Earl of Sutherland and, when he died, Alexander Ogilvie of Boyne.

Not long after the Queen's arrival in England after the Battle of Langside, she wrote to the Laird of Smeaton thanking him for his support and promising to repay all the money and effort he had expended on her behalf. She looked for support in her exile from Elizabeth the English Queen and, that failing, help from France (**fig. 42**).

41. *James Hepburn, 4th Earl of Bothwell (about 1535–78)* and
Lady Jean Gordon, Countess of Bothwell (1546–1629)
both oil on copper, dated 1566
by an unknown artist

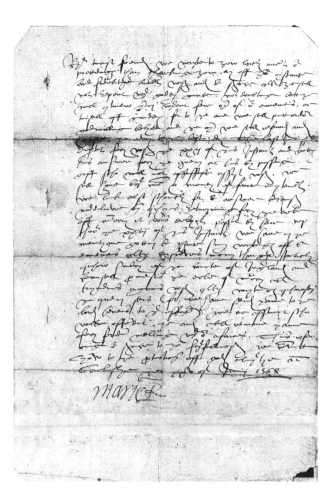

42. *Letter by Mary, Queen of Scots to the Laird of Smeaton*
Carlisle, 25 June 1568

In the second decade of the seventeenth century, James VI attempted to rehabilitate his mother's reputation. A number of portraits of Mary in later life exist which are typically Jacobean and must have been painted as an aspect of this policy. The portrait shown at the beginning of this chapter (**fig. 26**) was recorded as being at Cobham as early as 1672 and may have been painted for the King's cousin, Ludovic Stewart, 2nd Duke of Lennox. The head is partly based on a contemporary miniature by Nicholas Hilliard.

The original of this type of portrait, which may be the example at Hardwick Hall (probably painted by Rowland Lockey), was mistakenly believed to have been painted while Mary was a prisoner in Sheffield Castle. For that reason they are often called the 'Sheffield' type.

The cameo illustrated (**fig. 43**) is one of several of the Queen to have survived and could have been commissioned by Mary from France or Italy for distribution to friends and supporters. The Scottish goldsmith who made this heart-shaped pendant incorporated both the cameo and its original gold enamelled mount. He decorated his work with diamonds and a ruby.

[47]

43. *Gold enamelled locket set with a cameo of Mary, Queen of Scots*
late sixteenth century

44. *The Penicuik Jewels*
late sixteenth century

The Penicuik Jewels (**fig. 44**) were long preserved by the Clerks of Penicuik as relics of Mary, Queen of Scots. A member of the family had married a granddaughter of Giles Mowbray, one of the Queen's servants in her English imprisonment. It is possible that the necklace is made from the gold filigree beads of the bracelets given by the Queen to Giles just before her death. The gold enamelled locket with painted miniatures of a man and a woman is one of a small group of similar pieces made in Scotland to commemorate Mary and perhaps her son, or one of her husbands.

45. *James VI and I*
miniature on vellum
by Isaac Oliver
Lent by the Buchanan Society

James VI and I
1566–1625

JAMES VI was born in a small room in Edinburgh Castle on 19 June 1566, between ten and eleven in the morning. 'God has given you and me a son, begotten by none but you,' Mary, Queen of Scots told her husband. Less than eight months later, Lord Darnley was murdered at Kirk o' Field and two months after that the baby Prince saw his mother for the last time. While she was a prisoner in Lochleven Castle he was crowned King of Scots. He was just thirteen months old.

Brought up by the Earl of Mar in Stirling Castle, he studied Latin and Greek, French and Italian, theology, history and science. After a childhood disrupted by the struggles of the nobility vying for control of him, he began to rule for himself, with shrewdness and skill. His chief objective

47. James Douglas,
4th Earl of Morton
(about 1516–81)
oil on canvas
by Arnold Bronckorst

49. George Buchanan
(1506–82)
oil on panel, dated 158.
attributed to
Arnold Bronckorst

46. Oak carved armchair
Lent by the Earl
of Mar and Kellie

48. *James VI and I*
oil on panel
by Arnold Bronckorst

When James VI was a baby, he was sent to be 'nursit and upbrocht' by Annabella Drummond, Countess of Mar, and there is a chair reputed to be her nursing chair (**fig. 46**). The tall back, curving arms and heavy stretchers are typical of the *caquetcuse* or gossip chair, a distinctively Scottish style which developed from earlier French examples in the sixteenth century. This form of chair was generally, though not exclusively, of east coast of Scotland manufacture. The Earl of Mar died in 1572, but the Countess continued to have charge of the young King until 1577.

51. *Medal commemorating the marriage of James VI*
silver, 1590

50. *Communion cup, from Rosneath Kirk, Dumbartonshire*
by John Mossman, Edinburgh, 1585–6

When James VI was a child Scotland was ruled by a series of Protestant regents, one of whom was the Earl of Morton (**fig. 47**). The portrait appears to have been painted shortly before the spring of 1578, when he fell from power. It has elements of northern mannerism in its style. The twisted curtain, the pillar, the fanciful castle, quite unlike Morton's actual castle at Aberdour, and even the gestures of the arms are all conventions from that type of painting. Bronckorst, the artist, had initially come to Scotland from London to prospect for gold. He first came into contact with the Earl when he negotiated unsuccessfully for the removal from Scotland of the gold he had managed to mine. Three years later Morton was dead,

executed on the Maiden, the guillotine he himself had introduced into Scotland.

James was served by the painter Arnold Bronckorst from 1580 to 1583. The portrait of the King 'fra the belt upward' (**fig. 48**) is probably that for which Bronckorst received payment in 1580. James, looking childlike for a boy in his early teens, bears a male sparrowhawk on his left hand, indicative of his interest in hawking. The picture initially belonged to his tutor, Robert Young, who later gave it to James's son, Charles I. The latter's cipher is branded on the back of the panel.

Also Book of common order & psalter about 1579 (see note)

[52]

was to retain the friendship of Queen Elizabeth, so that he might succeed her, and when she signed his mother's death warrant in 1587 he made only a formal protest. Two years later, he married Anne of Denmark, a slim, fair-haired fourteen-year-old. Initially happy, they had three sons and four daughters, but they gradually drifted apart.

In 1603 James achieved his ambition and inherited the throne of England. He immediately moved south and established his court in London. He would have liked his two kingdoms to be completely united

52. *James VI and I and Anne of Denmark (1574–1619)* oil on circular panels attributed to Adrian Vanson

From 1570 to 1578 the young James VI had as tutor George Buchanan (**fig. 49**), a scholar and poet of distinction and an implacable enemy of Mary, Queen of Scots. In his youth he had tutored the famous French philosopher Montaigne in Bordeaux, and later corresponded with the astronomer Tycho Brahe. The inscription on the portrait reads, appropriately: 'Such is the face, so he bore his countenance. If you wish a sound mind, seek to know literature and the heavens.'

A very early example of a cup used by the recently reformed Church for its communion services (**fig. 50**) may originally have been a

secular wine cup. Its maker, John Mossman, was a member of a family of goldsmiths in Edinburgh, one of whom had been responsible for the re-making of the Scottish Crown in 1540. He was admitted as a master of the Incorporation of Goldsmiths in 1576 and was still working in 1592.

When James's prospective bride, Anne of Denmark, was delayed by contrary winds from making the voyage to Scotland, the impatient James took ship and spent the winter in Scandinavia before returning with her in May 1590. A medal (**fig. 51**) was struck to commemorate their wedding. On the obverse appear the busts of James and Anne.

but Scotland retained its own parliament, established church and legal system, and his policy of encouraging the Scottish and English nobility to intermarry met with little success. He liked to boast that he now ruled Scotland with a stroke of his pen, but in England he had inherited grave economic and religious problems from his predecessor. He grew prematurely old, his health failed and, living apart from his wife, he became ever more reliant on his favourite, the Duke of Buckingham. He came back to Scotland only once, in 1617, but the visit was marred by ecclesiastical disagreements. He died on 27 March 1625.

53. Gold four-pound pieces 1591–2

54. Silver half-merk 1591

In 1583 Adrian Vanson succeeded Bronckorst as principal painter at the Scottish court and was active until 1602. He was probably the only artist in the country at that time capable of sophisticated portraiture. Though miniature in size, the two little roundels of James and his Queen (**fig. 52**) are painted in a normal oil technique. That of the King relates closely to a full-size portrait which is dated 1595. The two panels are turned from single pieces of wood and their sections interlock, suggesting that they originally formed a hinged box.

Known as hat pieces owing to their striking bust of the king with tall 'sugar-loaf' hat, James VI's gold four-pound coins (**fig. 53**) are perhaps more interesting for their reverse design showing the Scottish lion holding a sceptre up to a heavenly cloud where the name of God appears in Hebrew script. James is thus shown to have divine approval for his rule, a concept that was to be developed into the divine right of kings by his successor Charles I.

The sword and scales on the reverse of the silver half-merk (**fig. 54**) are typical attributes of justice. The Latin inscription reads: 'In these things a tyrant differs from a king'. James wished to advertise his own just rule and show how fit he was for yet further kingly responsibility.

55. Stained glass roundel
dated 1600

56. The Pitfirrane Goblet
late sixteenth century

Compared with other parts of Europe, in Scotland glass was rare in the medieval period and little has survived. There was hardly any demand for vessel glass but a brisk trade in window glass existed. A roundel (**fig. 55**) bearing the motto: 'In my Defenc[e] God me Defend', shows the royal arms of Scotland impaling those of Anne of Denmark. Whether imported or made locally, this roundel would have been cut, decorated and mounted by a glass wright, probably in a royal palace or associated church building.

The Pitfirrane Goblet (**fig. 56**) was probably made in the southern Netherlands in the late sixteenth century by migrant Venetian glassworkers: it is of the style known as *façon de Venise*. Said to be the goblet from which James VI drank in Dunfermline before setting out for London in 1603, it later passed into the hands of the family of Halkett of Pitfirrane, who lived near Dunfermline. Apart from its association with the King, it is significant because it reflects the commercial and cultural exchanges between Scotland and the Low Countries in the sixteenth century.

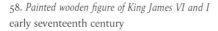
57. *Rosewater dish of pewter*
by Richard Weir, Edinburgh, 1603–25

58. *Painted wooden figure of King James VI and I*
early seventeenth century

In an age before the use of forks and table knives, dishes of scented water were placed on the dinner table so that diners could wash their hands. A rosewater dish of pewter (**fig. 57**) has a central brass plaque enamelled with the royal arms used by James VI after he became King of England. It may have been a royal gift, or was perhaps used in the royal household. The maker, Richard Weir, a member of the pewterers' craft, was admitted to the Edinburgh Incorporation of Hammermen, the trade organisation controlling all those who used a hammer in their work.

In a painted wooden figure of James (**fig. 58**) the King is represented crowned and enthroned, wearing his coronation robes. The figure has been designed so that his arm, probably once holding a sceptre, can be moved up and down by means of a lever projecting at the back. It may have formed part of some mechanical contrivance, like a clock.

After James's departure for London in 1603, John Graham, 3rd Earl of Montrose, was appointed the King's Commissioner for Scotland. He became James's representative in parliament and the General Assembly of the Church of Scotland. This commission granted him virtually vice-regal powers. He was heavily involved in the negoti-

59. *Seal box*
by George Cunningham, Canongate, 1604
Lent by the Duke of Montrose

60. *James VI and I*
oil on canvas, dated 1604
attributed to John de Critz

ations when James tried unsuccessfully to persuade his two parliaments to unite.

A silver-gilt box (**fig. 59**) was made to hold the wax impression of the Great Seal of Scotland which was fixed to the royal letter making the appointment. The seal box is engraved on one side with the royal arms as used in England, and on the other side with the Earl of Montrose's arms.

A number of portraits of James of the same basic type was produced in the earliest years of his reign in England. In a sense, they mark the union of the two crowns: the King is seen wearing in his hat the jewel known as the Mirror of Great Britain, which had been made up on his orders from the jewellery of Queen Elizabeth (**fig. 60**).

Variants of this portrait were produced between 1604 and 1618 in the studio of John de Critz the elder, one of a number of Anglo-Netherlandish artists active at the court in London. James disliked sitting for his portrait, which explains why this particular type was in vogue for so long.

The *Basilikon Doron*, 'The Kingly Gift' (**fig. 61**), was written by James VI in 1598 for his eldest son, Prince Henry, then aged four, as a book of advice in the principles of statecraft and the duties of a king. It

The left portion shows a facsimile of two printed pages:

MS ROYAL
18. B. xv.
fol. 1a.

To Henrie my dearest sonne and naturall successoure.[1]

Quhomto can sa richtlie[2] appartaine this booke of the institution of a prince in all the pointis of his calling als ueill generall,
as a christiane touardis god, as particulaire as a king touardis
his people : quhomto I saye can it sa iustlie appartaine as
unto you my dearest sonne, since I the authoure thairof as 5
youre naturall father man be cairfull for youre godlie &
uertuouse[3] education as my eldest[4] sonne and the first

[1] *Above this salutation there has been deleted the beginnings of two earlier attempts, to Henrie, and to my dearest.* [2] *ap deleted after richtlie.* [3] *r added above the line.* [4] *chylde deleted after eldest.*

WALDEGRAVE,
1599.

[sig. A4ᵃ]

TO *HENRIE* MY DEAREST SONNE AND NATVRAL SVCCESSOVR.

WHOME-TO can so rightly appertein this booke, of the
Institution of a Prince in all the poyntes of his calling,
as well generall (as a Christian towardes God) as particuler 10
(as a King towardes his people ?) whom-to (I say) can it so
iustlie apperteine, as vnto you my dearest Sonne ? Since I
the author thereof as your naturall Father, must be carefull
for your godlie and vertuous education as my eldest Sonne,
and the first fruites of Gods blessing towards me in my pos- 15
teritie : And (as a King) must timouslie prouide for your
[sig. A4ᵇ]
training vp in all the poyntes of a Kinges / office (since ye are
my naturall and lawfull Successour therein) that (being rightly
informed hereby of the weight of your burthen) yee may in
time begin to consider, that being borne to be a King, ye are 20
rather borne to ONVS, then HONOS : not excelling all your
people so far in rank and honour, as in daylie care and hazardous
paines-taking, for the duetifull administration of that greate
office that God hath layde vpon your shoulders : laying so a

61. *The Basilikon Doron*
1598

enshrined the generally accepted belief that monarchs were chosen by God, and the more particular instructions were directed at the problems of ruling Scotland. Drafted in his own 'unlegible and ragged hand', it was printed for private circulation the following year. It immediately aroused considerable interest throughout Western Europe, was translated into French, German, Dutch and Danish, and continued to be published. The copy illustrated is a modern composite edition by the Scottish Text Society.

James VI's eldest son, Henry Frederick, was a youth of exceptional promise – handsome, athletic, intelligent and popular. The portrait painted shortly after his arrival in London (**fig. 62**) is almost certainly the work of Robert Peake, who was appointed the Prince's principal painter. The ten-year-old boy is shown rather overwhelmed by the insignia of the Order of the Garter: the light blue garter below the knee, the collar made up of twenty-six garters, each with an enamelled rose in the centre, the dark blue velvet mantle lined with white taffeta and, on the table, the black velvet hat with ostrich feathers. Created Prince of Wales in 1610, Henry's brief life came to a sad end with his death from typhoid two years later.

Several variations of a medal (**fig. 63**), widely circulated among

63. *Prince Henry Frederick*
gold medal

62. *Henry Frederick, Prince of Wales*
(1594–1612)
oil on canvas, dated 1604
attributed to Robert Peake
Lent by the Earl of Mar and Kellie

64. *Lady Marie Stewart's Virginal*

Henry's friends, show a particularly fine portrait of the Prince, with his arms and personal motto: 'Glory is the light of an honourable mind' on the reverse.

In the sixteenth and seventeenth centuries the virginal was the household keyboard instrument and a vast amount of music was written for it. The strings were plucked rather than struck, and gave a compass of about four octaves. The virginal illustrated (**fig. 64**) is said to have belonged to Lady Marie Stewart, Countess of Mar, who was the second daughter of James VI's favourite cousin Esmé, Duke of Lennox. It is one of two surviving Scottish virginals, and may have

been made in the Low Countries, possibly in Antwerp. It is contained in a rectangular case of oak whose painted decorations include a classical scene of unicorn, lion, elephant and peacock listening to the playing of Orpheus.

Arabella Stewart (**fig. 65**) was the daughter of Lord Darnley's younger brother, Charles, and a first cousin of King James VI. This portrait's traditional identification as Arabella is given some support by its similarity to the features in the only certain portrait, a full-length at Hardwick Hall. A dog is usually a symbol of fidelity and the watch, dated 1605 inside the lid, is a reminder of mortality.

66. *Lady Arabella Stewart*
silver medal, about 1611

65. *Lady Arabella [Arbela] Stewart (1575–1615)*
oil on panel (oval), dated 1605
attributed to Marcus Gheeraerts

The unfortunate Arabella, sharing the King's descent from Margaret Tudor, had always been the object of grave suspicion because of her closeness to both the Scottish and the English thrones. Brought up in England, she was the centre of intrigue and plots to marry her off. On his removal to England James at first treated her well but on her secret marriage in 1610 against his wishes, to William Seymour, who also had a claim to the English throne, she was imprisoned. She died in the Tower of London in 1615. The medal illustrated (**fig. 66**) is a heartfelt plea from prison for 'God's ... patience' for one who 'dare not seek relief'.

King James is depicted in the portrait at the beginning of the chapter (**fig. 45**) wearing the George of the Order of the Garter on a bright blue ribbon which exactly matches the background. It has been suggested that this miniature is by Nicholas Hilliard rather than by Isaac Oliver, but in fact there are traces of Oliver's typical signature in the crook of the King's right arm. Oliver, related by marriage to both the de Critz and the Gheeraerts families of painters, was attached to the household of Anne of Denmark and the miniature may have been made on her behalf.

[60]

67. Alexander Seton, 1st Earl of Dunfermline
(about 1557–1622)

oil on canvas, dated 1610

by Marcus Gheeraerts

68. Robert Ker's silver-cased watch

by David Ramsay, about 1615

Alexander Seton, 1st Earl of Dunfermline (**fig. 67**), was Chancellor of Scotland from 1606 and was made a member of the English Privy Council in 1610, the probable occasion for the production of this portrait. Despite his Roman Catholic leanings, he was close to James and was given charge of his son, the future Charles I, when the King and Queen departed for London in 1603. Dunfermline's ascetic appearance is perhaps a reminder of his early education by Jesuits in Rome. The key at his wrist is likely to be a symbol, but its meaning is not clear.

Marcus Gheeraerts was the most forward-looking of the painters at court, and this is his masterpiece.

Robert Ker, 1st Earl of Somerset, was one of James VI's Scottish favourites. A younger son of Sir Thomas Ker of Ferniehirst, he followed James to England in 1603, becoming a Knight of the Garter and Lord High Treasurer of Scotland.

It was traditionally believed that the watch illustrated (**fig. 68**) was given to Ker by James. The dials show hours, date, phases of the moon and signs of the zodiac. The silver covers are engraved with scenes showing the Last Supper, Robert Ker's arms, the royal arms and James with his wife, Anne of Denmark. David Ramsay, the maker of the watch, also followed James to London and was appointed Chief Clockmaker to the King.

69. *Gold and enamelled badge
of a Baronet of Nova Scotia*

70. *James VI and I*
oil on canvas
by Adam de Colone

James VI instituted an Order of Baronets as a means of raising funds and encouraging the colonisation of Nova Scotia. The new hereditary knights could buy this honour for 2000 merks. James died before he could create any of the new baronets, and so the first was appointed by Charles I. As part of their privileges, they were allowed to wear the distinctive badge (**fig. 69**) on a yellow ribbon round the neck. This example belongs to a family whose baronetcy dates to 1634, but the badge itself was probably made in London, about 1780.

A new type of portrait of James VI (**fig. 70**) was painted in the last years of his life. This one is a reduced version of two full-lengths (now at Hatfield and Newbattle Abbey) for which the artist, Adam de Colone, received payment at Whitehall in July 1623. The format is based on a portrait of 1618 by the Netherlandish painter Van Somer, but it is likely that De Colone had fresh sittings from the King. The painter, Scottish-born, though of Netherlandish parents, was active in both Scotland and England from 1622 until 1628 when he seems to have settled in the Low Countries.

Charles I
1600–49

BORN at Dunfermline in 1600, James VI's second son Charles was brought up at the English court after his father inherited Elizabeth's throne. In early childhood he was very much overshadowed by his handsome, popular elder brother, Prince Henry Frederick, and his lively sister, Princess Elizabeth. A delicate child, he did not learn to walk until special supporting boots were made for him, and he had an inhibiting stammer, but he was also possessed of great determination and by the time he was in his teens he was an accomplished horseman and an energetic

72. *Queen Henrietta Maria (1609–69)* oil on canvas from the studio of Sir Anthony van Dyck

73. *Elizabeth, Queen of Bohemia (1596–1662)* oil on panel from the studio of Gerrit Honthorst

A portrait of Charles by the Dutch painter Daniel Mytens (**fig. 71**) shows him as a young man, beardless and still Prince of Wales. It is relatively domestic in pose, costume and setting. The picture was probably painted in 1623, shortly before his journey to Spain to woo the Infanta. It was when he saw the fashions at the Spanish court that he grew the small, pointed beard so characteristic of his later portraits. The first version of this painting was intended as a gift for the Infanta's father. Mytens, who had come to London from Holland in 1618, represents the more sophisticated generation of Netherlandish painters who superseded Gheeraerts and de Critz. His grasp of three-dimensional form and 'everyday' realism was greater than

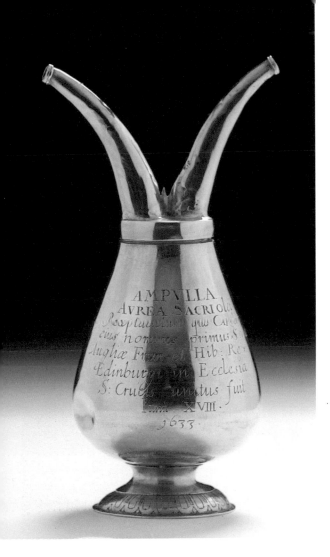

75. *Medals commemorating Charles I's Scottish Coronation*
1633

74. *Gold Ampulla used at the Scottish Coronation of Charles I*
1633

Elizabeth, elder sister of Charles I, married Frederick V, the Protestant Elector Palatine who shortly afterwards accepted the crown of Bohemia. He and Elizabeth ruled there during the winter of 1619–20. After their expulsion by the Catholic League she was often referred to as 'the Winter Queen'. Widowed in 1632, she spent most of her life in exile at the Orange court in The Hague. Many portraits of her were painted in the studios of Miereveldt and Honthorst. The earliest, by Miereveldt, invariably show her with a bare forehead, while in those by Honthorst (fig. 73), she seems always to wear a fringe.

The Scottish coronation of Charles took place at Holyroodhouse, Edinburgh, on 18 June 1633. A unique little phial (fig. 74) has a Latin inscription stating that it held the sacred anointing oil used during the coronation. Although it has no maker's mark, it may possibly have been made by James Dennistoun, Deacon of the Edinburgh Incorporation of Goldsmiths. A contemporary account of the coronation, by the Lord Lyon, Sir James Balfour, mentions that he carried the golden ampulla. It was preserved for generations in the family of Suttie of Balgone and it has been suggested that it had been commissioned by the City Treasurer, George Suttie, who retained it after the event.

theirs. In time, the King would come to prefer the glamour of Sir Anthony van Dyck, with his reminders of the great Renaissance paintings that Charles so loved.

Henrietta Maria and her children were painted many times by Van Dyck and, despite the rather artificial grandeur of the setting in the portrait illustrated (fig. 72), the Queen's vivacity and charm are evident. The original of this picture was probably painted in 1636 for a royal portrait gallery at Henrietta's palace, Somerset House. The portrait of Charles likely to have been its companion is still in the Royal Collection and bears that date.

tennis-player. In 1612, his elder brother died and his sister left England to marry Frederick of Bohemia. His father's favourite, Buckingham, befriended him, and under his cheerful influence Charles gradually lost his nervousness of his shrewd, outspoken father and grew in confidence. After an abortive attempt to marry him to the Spanish Infanta, he married the French Roman Catholic princess Henrietta Maria.

Their proxy wedding took place a few weeks after James's death, but at first the marriage was not a success. Homesick, Henrietta felt excluded by her husband's reliance on Buckingham, while he thought her pettish and impertinent. With the assassination of Buckingham in 1628 their relationship improved dramatically. They fell deeply in love, and there then ensued an idyllic interlude while their children were born and they presided over an elegant, sophisticated court.

Highly-educated, introspective and devoted to fine paintings, Charles seemed oblivious to the growing troubles around him. He had inherited his father's grave financial and political problems, and his attempts to bring the Church of Scotland into uniformity with the Episcopalian Church of England ended in disaster. He saw all Presbyterians as dangerous radicals, seditiously challenging his divine right to rule and he quickly lost control of the situation. Civil War broke out in both his kingdoms. After his defeat at Naseby, he surrendered to the Scots, but they handed him over to his English enemies and despite a Scottish attempt to rescue him in 1648, he was executed at Whitehall on 30 January 1649.

76. Falkland Palace and the Howe of Fife
oil on panel
by Alexander Keirincx

Gold and silver medals (**fig. 75**) were struck to commemorate Charles's Scottish coronation which show the King crowned and in his coronation robes, wearing collars of the Garter and Thistle. The reverse design has a thistle and rose tree combined. Some of the gold medals have an edge inscription indicating that they are made from Scottish gold. Curiously, some of the silver medals, like the one illustrated, have the same inscription. The medals were minted in Edinburgh by Nicholas Briot, a Frenchman, who was ordered to Scotland for this purpose. In the coronation procession on 18 June these gold and silver medals were thrown to the crowd by the Bishop of Moray.

Falkland Palace (**fig. 76**) was a favourite royal residence of the Stewarts. This painting of it includes the earliest known view of the Scottish countryside and is one of a series of ten painted for Charles I to record his 'houses & townes in Scotland'. It seems likely that the Netherlandish landscape painter Keirincx was commissioned to paint them in the years between Charles's triumphal entry into Edinburgh in 1633 and the growing 'troubles' in 1640. The land in the foreground is patterned by the ridge-and-furrow system of ploughing which preceded underground drainage. Beyond the palace is the famous royal deer park, protected by long fences and ditches, shortly afterwards to be destroyed by Cromwell.

Another painting in the series shows Seton Palace and the earliest known depiction of the Scottish coast (**fig. 77**). The medieval and Renaissance palace of the Seton family, frequently visited by the Stewarts, was a building of great complexity. After periods of decay, it was totally demolished in 1789. In the trees to the right of the palace is the truncated steeple of the collegiate church of St Mary and Holy Cross, which still stands.

By the early seventeenth century the growing city of Edinburgh had been divided into eight parishes, some based on older churches. The old Trinity College, founded about 1460 by Mary of Gueldres, widow of James II, became the parish kirk of the north-east quarter of the city in 1584. In 1632–3 it acquired a remarkable set of communion and baptismal silver including the plate of which a detail is illustrated **fig. 78**). The engraving on the plate shows a table set for communion with these silver vessels. It shows a man kneeling to take the Sacrament, a practice introduced by James VI in 1621 through the regulations known as the Five Articles of Perth. Charles I tried to enforce these as part of his campaign for ecclesiastical uniformity.

The imposition by Charles I of the *Book of Common Prayer* (**fig. 79**) on their Church was the last straw for many Scots. There were riots in the Edinburgh churches when it was first read on 23 July and this discontent and Charles's intransigence led to the signing of the

77. *Seton Palace and the Firth of Forth*
oil on panel; by Alexander Keirincx

National Covenant in 1638 and civil war. The prayer book was printed in Edinburgh in 1637 by the King's printer, Robert Young, and is bound with the 1636 edition of the Psalms of David translated by James VI. The binding has the Scottish Arms of Charles II.

James, 1st Duke of Hamilton, was Charles I's leading Scottish adviser and a close friend. He tried to reconcile him to the Scottish Covenanters and was sent as commissioner to the Glasgow General Assembly of 1638, but his attempts at moderation failed and he was eventually executed at Whitehall five weeks after the King.

His portrait (fig. 80) was painted by Daniel Mytens shortly after he and his wife, Lady Mary Feilding, had taken up residence in London.

This is one of the finest of British seventeenth-century portraits. Its harmonies of pale blue, grey and white are all parts of a studied informality. Mytens had painted a quite different, but equally beautiful, portrait of Hamilton five years earlier. Such is their quality that they suggest some special sympathy between the sitter and the artist.

Desperate for allies, Charles I reluctantly agreed to allow his nine-year-old daughter Mary to marry the young son of the Prince of Orange, whom he privately regarded as being too lowly in status to make a suitable husband for the Princess. A silver medal (fig. 81) was struck in Holland to celebrate their betrothal, and the wedding took place privately in April 1641.

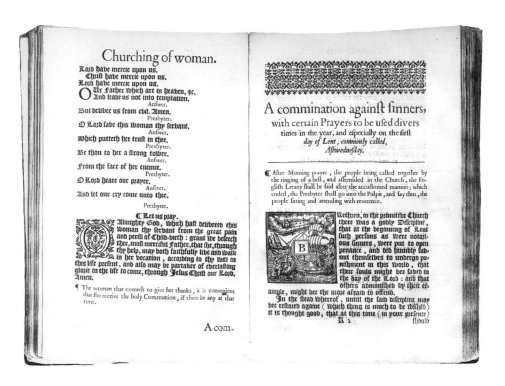

Churching of woman.

Lord have mercie upon us,
Christ have mercie upon us,
Lord have mercie upon us,
Our Father which art in heaven, &c.
And leade us not into temptation.
Answer.
But deliver us from evil. Amen.
Presbyter.
O Lord save this woman thy servant,
Answer.
Which putteth her trust in thee.
Presbyter.
Be thou to her a strong tower.
Answer.
From the face of her enemie.
Presbyter.
O Lord heare our prayer.
Answer.
And let our cry come unto thee.
Presbyter.
¶ Let us pray.

Almighty God, which hast delivered this woman thy servant from the great pain and perill of Child-birth : grant we beseech thee, most merciful Father, that she, through thy help, may both faithfully live and walk in her vocation, according thy will in this life present, and also may be partaker of everlasting glorie in the life to come, through Jesus Christ our Lord. Amen.

¶ The woman that cometh to give her thanks , it is convenient that she receive the holy Communion, if there be any at that time.

A com-

A commination against sinners,

with certain Prayers to be used divers times in the year, and especially on the first day of Lent, *commonly called,* *Ashwednesday.*

¶ After Morning prayer, the people being called together by the ringing of a bell, and assembled in the Church, the English Letany shall be said after the accustomed manner : which ended, the Presbyter shall go into the Pulpit, and say thus, the people sitting and attending with reverence.

Brethren, in the primitive Church there was a godly Discipline, that at the beginning of Lent such persons as were notorious sinners, were put to open penance, and did humbly submit themselves to undergo punishment in this world, that their souls might bee saved in the day of the Lord : and that others admonished by their example, might bee the more afraid to offend.

In the stead whereof , untill the said discipline may bee restored againe (which thing is much to be wished) it is thought good, that at this time (in your presence) should

R 2

79. *Prayer book from the Chapel Royal, Holyroodhouse* 1637

78. *Communion bread plate, from Trinity College Kirk* by Thomas Kirkwood, Edinburgh, 1633–5
detail of engraving
Lent by the Kirk Session of the Holy Trinity Church, Edinburgh

James Graham, 1st Marquis of Montrose, was originally a supporter of the Covenanters who opposed Charles, but he changed to the King's side in 1641. He was in Oxford between August 1643 and March 1644 when the portrait illustrated (**fig. 82**) and another, more allegorical one, must have been painted. Although it has warlike trappings it has a contemplative air, a reminder that Montrose was a distinguished poet as well as a great commander. His efforts on behalf of the youthful Charles II were to lead to his execution in Edinburgh in 1650.

The painter William Dobson's short career is almost completely associated with the court established by Charles I at Oxford when he was unable to regain possession of London. The artist's style suggests

[69]

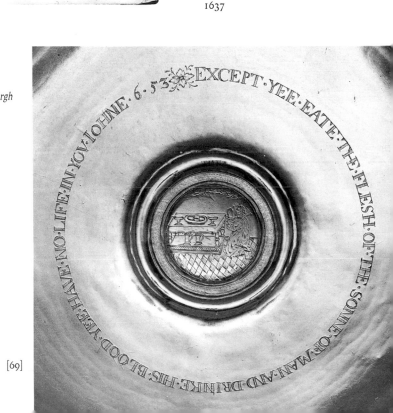

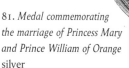

80. *James, 1st Duke of Hamilton (1606–49)*
oil on canvas, 1629
by Daniel Mytens

81. *Medal commemorating the marriage of Princess Mary and Prince William of Orange* silver

an earlier knowledge of the King's great collection of Venetian paintings.

Charles was executed on 30 January 1649 on a scaffold erected in front of his Banqueting House in Whitehall (**fig. 83**). The event was depicted in many contemporary engravings and in a number of paintings, all produced on the continent. Much of the detail of the picture must have been gleaned from eye-witnesses, although the representation of the building is wildly inaccurate. However, the need to show the event as a kind of martyrdom must have been the main aim of whoever commissioned the painting. There is even a hint of a parallel with Christ, for the horseman and, especially, the

82. *James Graham,*
1st Marquis of Montrose (1612–50)
oil on canvas
attributed to William Dobson

83. *The Execution of Charles I*
oil on canvas
by an unknown artist
Lent by the Earl of Rosebery

84. *Heart-shaped gold*
and enamelled pendant
about 1650

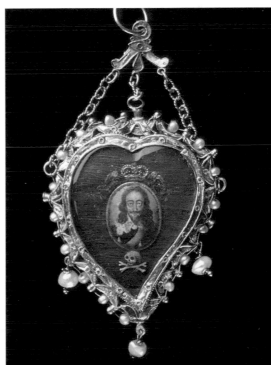

swooning woman, are common features of the iconology of the crucifixion. Charles's own portrait is opposed by that of Sir Thomas Fairfax, shown with axe in hand and presumably vilified in this way for his failure to prevent the King's execution.

A huge amount of memorial jewellery and mementoes was produced to commemorate the death of 'the Martyr King'. An exceptionally fine and rare example is the pendant locket which contains a miniature of Charles I, a lock of his hair and a fragment of the blood-stained linen shirt he wore at his execution (**fig. 84**). It belonged to Lady Jane Murray, daughter of the 1st Earl of Hartfell and wife of Sir William Murray of Stanhope, both noted royalists.

[71]

85. *Charles II*
oil on canvas
by William Dobson

Charles II
1630–85

CHARLES was born and brought up in St James's Palace, London. He was a large, solemn, black-haired child who resembled his mother's French relatives more than his father's Stewart ancestors. His life was dramatically disrupted when he was eight, with the outbreak of the Civil War. He was present at the battle of Edgehill, accompanying his father and his brother James. Later he was with the royal court at Oxford for some months, before Charles I ordered his son to seek the greater safety of the west country, Jersey and eventually France.

When his father was executed in 1649, the horrified Scots invited Charles to lead an army against the usurper, Cromwell. He arrived in the Cromarty Firth, was crowned at Scone in 1651 and marched south with his forces, only to be crushed at the battle of Worcester. Escaping in

86. Medal commemorating the Battle of Dunbar 1650

disguise, he returned to Paris once more, taller, tougher and sunk in melancholy.

For the next nine years he fought in continental armies and negotiated secretly with his supporters. When Cromwell finally died and his son Richard Cromwell showed no desire to govern in his place, Charles was able to claim his inheritance. He rode into London in triumph on his thirtieth birthday. Soon afterwards, he married the plump, devout Portuguese Catherine of Braganza, who fell in love with him and gradually learned to share him with his many mistresses.

Charles had a lively interest in scientific affairs and a cynical grasp of

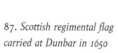
87. *Scottish regimental flag carried at Dunbar in 1650*

88. *Medals commemorating Charles II's Coronation at Scone, 1651* gold and silver

The young Prince's portrait (**fig. 85**) was painted in about 1643 during the stay of his father's court in Oxford. The painting by William Dobson is replete with the symbolism of civil war. Charles, in front of the cracked pillar of fortitude, prepares to put on the helmet of war and declares his determination to fight for his father's cause. At his feet are the symbols of strife, the head of the Gorgon Medusa and the trumpet of the war-goddess Athena. The artist, one of the finest to work in Britain in the seventeenth century, painted almost exclusively for the royal court in the years 1642–6.

The year after Charles I's execution Cromwell marched north and on

3 September 1650 he defeated the Scots at the battle of Dunbar, gaining control of the country as far north as the River Forth. Until the day before the battle he had been totally out-generalled by the Scottish commander, David Leslie, and forced into a trap at Dunbar, with no means of escape except by sea. Leslie, however, was ordered into an unwise change of position by the all-powerful Committee of Estates which accompanied the army and saw fit to issue instructions as to how their general should conduct military affairs.

After their victory, Cromwell and his army wintered in Scotland and the following year were in complete control of the country. Fine medals by Thomas Simon were awarded to English soldiers who political realities. Recalling with distaste his days among the Scottish Presbyterians who had lectured him constantly about morality, he had no desire to go north again and he left it to his secretary of state, the Duke of Lauderdale, to enforce in Scotland his policies of royal absolutism in both church and state.

Although he had many illegitimate sons and daughters, Charles had no children by his Queen and so his brother, James, remained his heir. Like James, the King was suspected of being a Roman Catholic but, unlike his brother, he saw that he must conceal his true religion. Only on his deathbed did he acknowledge his allegiance to his mother's church.

89. *Trumpet Banner, embroidered with the arms of Charles II about 1660*

distinguished themselves in the battle (**fig. 86**). The obverse has a bust of Cromwell with the battle faintly visible in the background and the reverse a view of Parliament.

Among the Scottish troops fighting for Charles II at Dunbar was Colonel Scott's regiment. A flag of blue silk with a saltire (**fig. 87**) is said to have been the regiment's standard.

Invited back from exile to lead the Scots against Cromwell once again, Charles II was crowned at Scone on 1 January 1651. This was the last time a reigning Scottish king set foot in Scotland until 1822.

On the obverse of the commemorative medals struck for the occasion (**fig. 88**), the King is crowned and wears coronation robes. On the reverse a lion rampant grasps a thistle in its paw. Another ten years would pass before Charles could be crowned in England.

Banners would have hung from the trumpets of the four state trumpeters who announced the heralds when they were making official proclamations. The banner illustrated (**fig. 89**) was probably made in England, but it shows the royal arms of Charles II as used in Scotland. Trumpeters with banners of this kind can be seen on the engraving of the Riding of Parliament (**fig. 118**).

90. *Charles II*
engraved after Sir Godfrey Kneller, dated 1679
by Robert White

91. *Catherine of Braganza (1638–1705)*
oil on canvas
by an unknown artist

The King was first introduced to the painter Sir Godfrey Kneller in 1678 by his own illegitimate son, the Duke of Monmouth. The resulting portrait is now lost, but its appearance is known from a preparatory drawing and Robert White's engraving (**fig. 90**), which was published the following year.

Catherine, daughter of John, King of Portugal, married Charles II in 1662. The diarist John Evelyn found her pretty, but her principal attractions in England were the overseas possessions, money and trading privileges in Portugal that she brought as a dowry. Her failure to provide an heir was a grave disadvantage and her Roman Catholi-

cism led to accusations of treason, but Charles was loyal to her, in his way. After his death she returned to Portugal, ruling for a time as regent for her nephew. Her favourite painter was Jacob Huysmans, a Roman Catholic from Antwerp. The portrait illustrated (**fig. 91**) has some of his rather mannered, 'metallic' qualities, and may have come from his studio.

Catherine of Braganza is also depicted in a carved agate cameo on the back of a gold and enamel scent bottle (**fig. 92**). On the front is a miniature of Charles II. Both pictures cover small compartments for cosmetics.

92. *Gold and painted enamel scent bottle* about 1670

93. *Mary, Princess of Orange (1631–60)*
oil on canvas, dated 1659
by Adriaen Hanneman

Mary, Princess of Orange (**fig. 93**) was widowed just before the birth of her only son William (later William II and III) in 1650. She devoted herself to securing his rights as well as those of her adored brother, Charles II, who was restored in 1660, the year after this portrait was painted. These aims seem to be expressed in the strangely protective gesture she makes over the little crown. She joined Charles in London at the Restoration, only to die of smallpox that winter

Charles's youngest and favourite sister was Henrietta Anne (**fig. 94**). 'Minette' ('Little Puss') as Charles II called her, was born at the

height of the Civil War. She was left behind by her mother when Henrietta Maria fled to France to seek help for the Royalist cause. Her governess later managed to escape with her from England and she was brought up in Paris by her mother. She went to London briefly after the Restoration but she was already engaged to her cousin Philippe, Duke of Orleans, brother of Louis XIV, and she returned to France to marry him. She later acted as intermediary in the negotiations for the Secret Treaty of Dover between Charles and Louis, allying Britain and France against the Dutch. She died of peritonitis in 1670.

The head in the portrait illustrated is close to many portraits

[77]

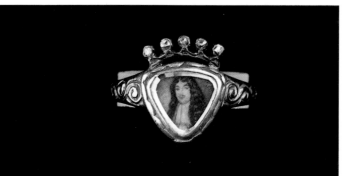

94. *Henrietta Anne, Duchess of Orleans (1644–70)*
oil on canvas
from the studio of Pierre Mignard

96. *Archbishop Sharpe's Night Clock*
by Joseph Knibb,
London, about 1670

95. *Gold ring set with diamonds*, about 1670

usually attributed to Pierre Mignard. It was painted for the Earl of Clarendon and must originally have hung with Lely's portraits of the Duke and Duchess of York (**figs 100, 101**).

A great many commemorative rings were produced to promote the later Stewart monarchs, ranging in quality from the crude to the very fine, such as the one shown (**fig. 95**). Under the triangular, table-cut diamond is a miniature of Charles II and the back is engraved with the initials CR for *Carolus Rex* [King Charles].

The Presbyterians abolished bishops from the Church of Scotland in Charles I's reign, but Charles II reintroduced them after the Restoration in 1660. Archbishop Sharpe at first opposed this move, but he

97. *John Maitland,*
Duke of Lauderdale (1612–82)
oil on canvas
by Sir Peter Lely

later changed his mind and accepted the position of Archbishop of St Andrews. Extreme Covenanters considered him to be a traitor to their cause, and a group of them murdered him on 3 May 1679 as he was crossing Magus Moor, near St Andrews, in his coach.

The clock illustrated (**fig. 96**) is thought to have been acquired by Archbishop Sharpe, during one of his visits to London. It is spring-driven, with three small oil lamps inside the case, which shine through the cut-out figures in the face so that the time can be read in the dark.

John Maitland, Duke of Lauderdale (**fig. 97**), was Secretary for Scotland from the Restoration until 1680, and was the virtual ruler of Scotland in these years. This portrait has all the sumptuous colour

and supple handling of paint of Sir Peter Lely at his finest with, in addition, an exceptional feeling for Lauderdale's character. Bishop Burnet, who knew him personally, described him in terms that the portrait confirms: 'He was very big: his hair red, hanging oddly about him [in the portrait he wears a wig]: his tongue was too big for his mouth, which made him bedew all that he talked to.'

Lauderdale is said to have given a silver girdle, or woman's belt (**fig. 98**), to Margaret Hardie of Midside Farm, the wife of one of his tenants. She had kept paying her rents while he was imprisoned by Cromwell in the Tower of London in the 1650s, and after the Restoration the Duke rewarded her loyalty with this gift.

98. *Midside Maggie's Girdle*
by Adam Allan, Edinburgh, 1608–10

99. *Silver seal box*
by Thomas Ker, Edinburgh

Sir Alexander Don of Newton was granted 'the title and dignity of Knight baronet of the Kingdom of Scotland' on 7 June 1667. About thirty years later a box (**fig. 99**) was made to hold the wax impression of the Great Seal of Charles II which is fixed to the charter. One side is engraved with the royal arms as used in Scotland between 1660 and 1688, and the other has the arms and motto of Sir Alexander Don. The engraver seems to have made a mistake with the heraldic colour code for the family arms as they are not those now recognised for the Dons.

100. *James, Duke of York, later James VII and II*
oil on canvas
by Sir Peter Lely

James VII and II
1633–1701

LIKE Charles II, James grew up amidst the turmoil of civil war. He was captured when Oxford surrendered to the parliamentary army, but he managed to escape to Holland disguised as a girl, and from there he travelled to Paris to join his mother. Both he and she were quick-tempered and obstinate, and after one particularly violent quarrel he ran away to enlist in the army. He served with distinction under the French Marshal Turenne, then fought in the Spanish forces in Flanders. His return to England at the Restoration was somewhat marred by his revelation that he had secretly married Anne, daughter of the Lord Chancellor, Sir Edward Hyde, later Earl of Clarendon. She was not of high enough rank, his family thought, but she was now eight months pregnant and so they were forced to accept her. Charles had made James Lord High Admiral, and he carried out his duties enthusiastically. However, his declaration in 1669 that he had converted to Roman Catholicism plunged the King and himself into deep difficulties. By now a widower, he made matters even worse the following year by marrying the Roman Catholic Mary Beatrice of Modena.

British Protestants were highly alarmed at the prospect of James inheriting his brother's throne, and Charles found it prudent to send him into exile twice, to the Hague and then to Scotland in 1679 and 1680 as Lord High Commissioner. His stay at Holyrood saw a resurgence in cultural activities in Edinburgh with the return of a royal court, but his Catholicism alienated the Scots irrevocably.

When he inherited the throne his attempts at introducing religious toleration were seen as sinister manifestations of his desire to convert his kingdoms to his own religion. The final crisis came when Mary Beatrice gave birth to a son and heir. Amidst rumours that the infant was someone else's child, smuggled into the royal bedchamber in a warming-pan, leading British statesmen invited James's Calvinist son-in-law William of Orange to rule with his wife instead, and James and his family fled. Defeated by William at the Battle of the Boyne, he died in exile in France eleven years later.

101. *Anne Hyde,*
Duchess of York (1637–71)
oil on canvas
by Sir Peter Lely

The marriage of James, Duke of York and Anne Hyde, was made public in December 1660. Two portraits to mark the marriage (**figs 100** and **101**) were commissioned for Anne's father, Sir Edward Hyde, created Earl of Clarendon by Charles II soon after the Restoration. The Duke and Duchess were great patrons of Sir Peter Lely, whose work was less popular with the King. Both portraits are highly complex arrangements of colour and light, showing Lely at his most baroque. By indicating the baton with an imperious finger, the Duke refers to his continental experience in the arts of war.

Behind the glamour and pomp of the two portraits lies the reality of the displeasure, and even horror, felt by the Duke's mother and Anne's father at the secret marriage in London in September 1660. Clarendon took the view that 'he had much rather his daughter should be the Duke's whore than his wife'. The urn and the fountain in the painting of Anne are allusions to love and purity. This portrait was seen before it was finished by Samuel Pepys the diarist in June 1662. Anne was to die of cancer at the age of thirty-four, leaving two surviving daughters, the future Queens Mary and Anne.

In 1686, James VII instructed his Lord Chancellor of Scotland, the Earl of Perth, to furnish the Abbey Church of Holyrood as his Roman Catholic Chapel Royal. Perth was given £8000 sterling for this

purpose and bought most of the necessary items in London. It is recorded (by a Protestant) that on 23 November 1686 'the King's Yaught arrived ... at Leith with the popish altar, vestments, images, priests and other dependers for the popish chapel in the abbey'.

The chapel was formally opened on St Andrews Day 1686. Two years later came the Revolution which deposed James and, on the night of 10 December, Holyroodhouse was attacked by a mob and the furnishings of the chapel were destroyed. Some of the altar plate was saved by David Burnet, one of the priests, who escaped with it to the predominantly Roman Catholic district of Enzie in Banffshire.

The altar plate (**fig. 102**) was dispersed, with certain pieces being used at Holyroodhouse in 1802, when the exiled French royal family were in residence there. The complete group was reunited in 1967 when the Scottish Roman Catholic Hierarchy and the Mother Superior of St Margaret's Convent, Edinburgh, deposited it in the Museum. The Altar Plate consists of a Monstrance used to expose the Host during the Mass; a Ciborium, used to hold the Host (both pieces having been made by a London silversmith with the mark WF); a Thurible or incense burner and an Incense Boat, both made by 'GC' of London; an Incense Spoon, made by William Scott of Edinburgh, and possibly supplied by the Earl of Perth; a Chalice and Paten, which have no maker's mark; and a Sanctus Bell, rung at the

102. *The Holyrood
Altar Plate*
1686–7
*Lent by the
Rev. Mother Superior,
St Margaret's Convent,
Edinburgh, and The Scottish
Roman Catholic Hierarchy*

103. *Mary Beatrice
of Modena (1658–1718)*
oil on canvas, dated 1687
by Willem Wissing

most solemn part of the Mass, made by Zacharias Mellinus of Edinburgh. All these pieces, except the Spoon, are engraved with James VII's royal cipher.

James's second wife, Mary Beatrice, was the only daughter of Alfonso IV, Duke of Modena. She was married by proxy to James, Duke of York in September 1673, and first met him two months later, at Dover. His choice of an Italian, Roman Catholic bride significantly increased his unpopularity with British Protestants. In her portrait by Willem Wissing (fig. 103) she is seen with a parrot, prominently placed, in Counter-Reformation iconology an emblem of eloquence

and, by extension, the Word of God. The artist, who came from Holland in 1676, was Lely's most competent pupil.

A terracotta bust, possibly of North Italian origin (fig. 104), shows James wearing the collar and badge of the Order of the Garter. At the base of the bust is a blank escutcheon, surmounted by what appears to be a ducal coronet, the form of which the sculptor has not fully understood. The coronet implies that James is shown while still Duke of York.

The bust is not English, and is unlikely to be Netherlandish, although James was in The Hague and Brussels during 1679. If it is

*104. James VII and II
terracotta bust
by an unknown artist*

*105. Pattern sixty-shilling piece of James VII and II
1688*

North Italian, it could be connected with his marriage to Mary Beatrice in 1672, although he did not travel to Italy in person.

James revived the chivalric Order of the Thistle in May 1687. The collar of the order is shown surrounding the royal arms as used in Scotland on a sixty-shilling piece (**fig. 105**). Although dies for this coin were made in 1688, none was actually issued before James was deposed. This example was struck from the original dies in 1828.

William II and III
1650–1702
and *Mary II*
1662–94

107. *Mary II (1662–94)*
oil on canvas
from the studio of
Willem Wissing

WILLIAM of Orange had a double connection with the royal house of Stewart, for his mother was Mary, daughter of Charles I. She married the Prince of Orange at the beginning of the Civil War, and nine years afterwards, when she was in an advanced state of pregnancy, her young husband died of smallpox. Their son William was born a few days later. A delicate, undersized, asthmatic child, he was deeply attached to his mother. She also died of smallpox when he was eleven, and his courtiers were surprised at the depth of his grief. After a precarious childhood, he grew up obsessed with the need to defend his country against the ever-present menace of France on his southern borders. He led his army himself, and he worked hard at building up an anti-French alliance.

During those years he was on good terms with his uncles, Charles II and James VII, visiting them, corresponding with them regularly and, in 1677, marrying James's daughter Mary. As a Calvinist, he became increasingly disturbed by James's evident Roman Catholicism, and so he was ready to accept the British invitation to take the throne in place of James. He and his wife were declared joint rulers, first in England, where he became William III, and then in Scotland, where he was William II. Mary, who was devoted to him, was content to leave all affairs of state to him.

He never did visit Scotland, for he remained preoccupied with continental politics and warfare, frequently returning to Holland and building up a Grand Alliance against France. Although he was at first popular with

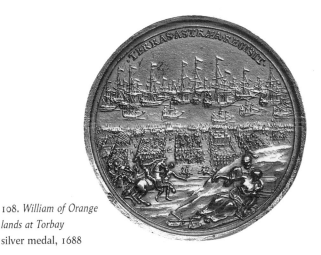

108. *William of Orange lands at Torbay* silver medal, 1688

109. *Coronation of William and Mary* silver medal, 1689

Sir Godfrey Kneller's portrait of William (**fig. 106**) was probably painted in the early 1690s. The suggestions of Roman gladiatorial costume refer to William's military prowess, and the pillar on the left is also decorated with trophies of war. So lively is the painting of the King's head that there is every likelihood that it was done from life. This is reinforced by a halo-like effect round the head, which suggests that it was painted in different circumstances from the rest of the canvas. The design of the head is the same as that in a full-length portrait in robes of state in the royal collection, which became a standard image.

Mary (**fig. 107**) did everything she could to enter into William's way of life and, when Queen, her warmth of character compensated for his withdrawn personality. In the summer of 1685 James VII had sent Willem Wissing back to Holland to paint his elder daughter and her husband. Constantine Huyghens saw Wissing, who had been a pupil of Lely, working on the portrait and remarked that he had not 'reached the perfection of his master'. The original of the painting, still in the royal collection, has a landscape background.

William arrived in England on 5 November 1688 in response to the invitation from the British Protestants. A medal was struck to the Presbyterian Scots, his severe treatment of the Jacobites who rose against him in 1689, his part in approving the Massacre of Glencoe of 1692 and his apparently callous disregard of the interests of those Scots trying to establish a trading venture at Darien led to widespread resentment.

William and Mary had no children, and she died in 1694. He therefore agreed to settle the succession on Anne, his wife's younger sister. He himself died after a fall from his horse in 1702.

110. *Wine glass engraved with a portrait of William of Orange about 1750*

111. *Wine goblet engraved with a portrait of William of Orange*

commemorate this event (**fig. 108**). Many medals were also struck to celebrate William and Mary's coronation in London on 21 April 1689 (**fig. 109**).

Glasses appropriately engraved were used for Protestant loyalist toasts long after the death of William in 1702. A glass (**fig. 110**) shows the King on horseback, framed with a scroll inscribed 'The Glorious Memory of King William', and commemorating the Battle of the Boyne with the words 'Boyne 1st July 1690'.

A wine goblet (**fig. 111**) also commemorates the battle of the Boyne and has garlands of vines and grapes and a similar inscription.

The wax bust of William by Anna Maria Braunin (**fig. 112**) was probably devised from painted portraits and engravings. The artist worked in Nürnberg and Frankfurt, and later at the Habsburg court in Vienna. She specialised in highly realistic wax miniature portraits and figurines, which appealed to central European taste. The bust is made up from waxes impregnated with various pigments, fabrics (partly coated in wax), pearls and, on the head, a wig of actual hair. The artist's characteristic signature is on a separate piece of wood fixed to the base of the box in which the bust sits.

112. *William II and III* polychrome wax bust by Anna Maria Braunin

113. *Pack of Heraldic Playing Cards* by Walter Scott, Edinburgh, 1691

114. *Bank note by the Company of Scotland* about 1696

A pack of fifty-three cards (**fig. 113**) features the Royal Arms of Scotland, the arms of the Lord Lyon and the arms of the peers of Scotland, including those of the eight original Knights of the Thistle. An 'introductory' card has the arms of Edinburgh, and an inscription showing that the pack was engraved by Walter Scott, an Edinburgh goldsmith.

In 1695 the Company of Scotland was set up to encourage Scottish overseas trade and colonisation. Empowered to trade with Africa, Asia and America, it was initially supported by King William and a large number of English financiers. However, pressure from other English vested interests, including the powerful East India Company, forced William to abandon his support and led to the withdrawal of all English and European capital. It was only after this reverse that the Company turned to the ambitious, but ultimately disastrous, 'Darien Scheme', which proposed the founding of a Scottish colony on the Isthmus of Panama, to control trade between the Atlantic and Pacific Oceans.

The Scots were ill-prepared for such a venture and William was determined not to provoke Spain, who claimed sovereignty of Darien. Failure in these circumstances was inevitable, and the venture ended with considerable loss of life, huge debts, and the

115. *Chest with elaborate lock mechanism*
late seventeenth century

116. *Gold Pistole and Half-pistole, William II*
1701

feeling in Scotland that William and his English government were to blame for the tragedy.

The Company had intended to exercise a variety of banking functions, including the issuing of notes. Whether it ever did so is unknown, as no contemporary notes have survived. Illustrated (**fig. 114**) is a 'pull' (proof) taken in the nineteenth century from the original printing plate.

A chest which probably held cash and important documents belonging to the Company of Scotland passed into the ownership of the Bank of Scotland. It remains in their possession, on display in the museum of their Head Office on the Mound, Edinburgh. The lid of the chest (**fig. 115**) was given to the National Museums by the Bank's Directors.

The ship *African Merchant* made the Company of Scotland's only successful voyage, bringing in a clear profit of £46,668 Scots from over seventy pounds (weight) of gold. The two coins illustrated (**fig. 116**) were minted from the gold – the last Scottish gold coins to be minted. They have the Company's crest of a rising sun underneath the King's head.

117. *Queen Anne*
oil on canvas
by Willem Wissing and
Jan van der Vaart

Anne
1665–1714

THE younger surviving daughter of James VII and Anne Hyde, Princess Anne had such poor sight that she was sent over to her grandmother in France when she was three so that she could be treated by Parisian eye specialists. At eighteen, she was married to Prince George, the younger brother of the King of Denmark. 'I have tried him drunk and tried him sober, and there is nothing in him', said Charles II. But Anne loved him dearly and she became pregnant seventeen times. Tragically, these pregnancies all ended with miscarriages, stillbirths, or the birth of children who did not survive early childhood. Only William, Duke of Gloucester, lived past his earliest years, but he had always suffered from hydrocephalus and he died five days after his eleventh birthday.

Two years later, in 1702, Anne inherited her brother-in-law's throne. She had visited Edinburgh when she was fifteen, enjoying the balls at Holyroodhouse when her father was Lord High Commissioner, but her poor health made it impossible for her to go north after she became Queen.

During her reign there took place one of the most momentous developments in Scottish history. Throughout the closing years of the seventeenth century, Scotland and England found it increasingly difficult to co-exist, for their parliaments had differing foreign and economic policies. Eventually, it seemed that the union of the crowns itself was in danger, for while England settled the succession on the Protestant Sophia of Hanover, Elizabeth of Bohemia's youngest daughter, and her heirs, the Scots declared that they were free to choose someone else if they so desired. Everyone realised that the situation was untenable and in 1707, after months of bitter debate, the Scottish parliament finally agreed that henceforth the United Kingdom of Great Britain would have one parliament only, sitting in London. Anne's health was already seriously undermined by her constant pregnancies, and she finally died in 1714. 'Sleep was never so welcome', wrote her doctor, 'to a weary traveller than death was to her.' Her cousin Sophia of Hanover had predeceased her and so it was Sophia's son who now ascended the throne as King George I, Britain's first Hanoverian monarch, while James VII's son continued to live in exile.

118. *The Riding of Parliament*
details from engraving,
1685

Anne's portrait (**fig. 117**) was probably painted soon after her marriage to Prince George of Denmark. It was then engraved in mezzotint by John Smith, who records that it was painted by Van der Vaart as well as by Wissing. The contribution of the former is likely to have been to the draperies. Unlike her later portraits, Anne is shown when she was still slim and attractive, her features having a youthful sensuality which may derive more from the artist's perception of her than from her own personality.

The final years of Scotland's separate parliament saw the members engage more actively in debate than ever before, as they argued over foreign policy, economic affairs and, above all, over their relationship with England. An engraving of 1685 shows the customary procession of the members from the royal Palace of Holyroodhouse to the Parliament House on 23 April. Drawn by Roderick Chalmers of Portlethen, Ross Herald and Herald Painter, it presents a graphic description of the cavalcade and ceremonies attending the 'down sitting' of the Scottish parliament before its disappearance under the terms of the Act of Union of 1707. Various acts of parliament regulated the ceremonial, the order of peers in the procession (**fig. 118**) and the privilege of bearing the Honours of Scotland (the Scottish Crown Jewels).

119. *The Downsitting of the Parliament*
engraving

The only known depiction of the Scottish parliament in session is an engraving published in the eighteenth century with figures in late seventeenth-century dress (**fig. 119**). Some details may have been taken from a sixteenth-century drawing. In the Middle Ages, parliament had comprised the 'Three Estates': the nobility, clergy and burgesses. The constituent membership changed after the Reformation with the transfer of religious titles to temporal lordships and, by the time the engraving was made, a fourth estate had been added, consisting of commissioners of the shire. The Scottish parliament was always a single chamber assembly, unlike its English counterpart. The picture shows the throne occupied by the monarch's representative, the Lord High Commissioner. The Honours of Scotland can also be seen.

James Francis Edward Stewart

('James VIII and III', 'The Old Pretender')
1688–1766

JAMES FRANCIS EDWARD Stewart was born on 10 June 1688, long after everyone had given up hope of Mary Beatrice bearing a living son. On 9 December, his mother disguised herself as a laundress, wrapped the baby up like a bundle of washing and crept out of the Palace of Whitehall with his two nurses, to escape to France. The exiled royal Stewarts were given the Palace of St Germain by Louis XIV, and there the child was brought up, along with his younger sister, Louisa Maria, born in 1692. Nine years later James VII suffered a stroke and, as he lay dying, Louis XIV promised to recognise his son as King James VIII and III. In 1713, however, Louis made peace with Britain and, as a result, James was forced to leave France, settling first in Avignon, then in Bologna and finally in Rome.

By that time, George I was on the British throne and James was well aware that exiled Jacobites looked to him to win back his rightful inheritance and theirs. He made an unsuccessful attempt to land in Scotland when he was just nineteen, but had to return ignominiously to France. After a period of service with the French army he tried again in 1715, joining the Earl of Mar's rising and establishing his court at Scone. Within a matter of weeks, however, he was forced to flee back to the continent.

By the time he was approaching thirty, his friends were desperate for him to marry and continue the Jacobite line, so in 1719 he married the Polish princess Clementina Sobieska. The birth of his two sons, Charles and Henry, encouraged his supporters but he himself had long since given up hope of leading a successful invasion of Britain and he stayed in his Muti Palace in Rome, writing letters constantly to his friends but growing more depressed with every month that passed. His enemies called him 'Old Mr Melancholy' and 'the Old Pretender' (Claimant). He died in 1788 without seeing Britain again.

121. *Prince James Francis Edward Stewart*
oil on canvas, dated 1691
by Nicholas de Largillièrre

Because of the slanders about the Prince's parentage, it was more than usually necessary that portraits should emphasise his identity. The large Prince of Wales feathers on the drapery in the background of his portrait by Largilliérre (**fig. 121**) serve this purpose. The King Charles spaniel, favourite breed of James's uncle, may also serve as a reminder that this child is a true Stewart prince.

Nicholas de Largillièrre had previously worked for James and Mary Beatrice in London. Now settled in Paris, he painted a number of portraits of James Francis Edward in the early 1690s. An engraving of one of these shows an identical head, and is inscribed 'Prince and Steward of Scotland'.

Medals were often used to convey political messages. The flight of the infant Prince James Francis Edward, carried in the arms of a Jesuit priest, mounted on a lobster, is shown on a silver medal of 1689 (**fig. 122**). The design has a satirical intent and also suggests that he was illegitimate.

James VII, who was promoting his son, James Francis Edward, as the true heir to his thrones, possibly had as many as seven thousand medals like the one illustrated (**fig. 123**) produced for propaganda purposes. This medal may have been struck either to influence the negotiations leading up to, or protesting against, the Treaty of Ryswick, which recognised William of Orange as British king.

122. *The Flight of Prince James*
silver medal, 1689

124. *James VIII and III*
silver medal, 1704

126. *Queen Anne and Prince James Francis Edward*
silver medal, 1710

123. *'The True-born Prince of Wales'*
silver medal, 1697

125. *The Attempted Invasion of Scotland*
silver medal, 1708

A silver medal of 1704 (**fig. 124**) was the first to be produced by the Jacobite court since 1699, and was also the first in which James is given his regal titles. His father, James VII, had died three years before.

Anti-English feeling ran high in Scotland immediately after the Union, and it was thought that an invasion of Scotland by the Jacobites would have a good chance of harnessing this discontent. The French invasion fleet was, however, driven away both by bad weather and the British Navy. A medal (**fig. 125**) was issued as propaganda to accompany this first attempt to recover James Francis Edward's throne by force.

A series of medals show the Stewart family. One of these (**fig. 126**) is possibly a reminder that James and Anne were half-brother and half-sister, although on opposing sides. It may, however, be a subtle piece of Whig propaganda. The medal, in its original case, is one of the relics of Sir John Hynde Cotton, leader of the English Jacobites.

Another satirical medal (**fig. 127**) pours scorn on the Jacobite attempts of 1708 and 1715.

In July 1717 the Hanoverian King George I granted a free pardon to all (with a few exceptions) who had been involved in the recent rebellions. This was commemorated by a medal (**fig. 128**) which praises his clemency.

128. *George I's Act of Grace*
bronze medal, 1717

130. *Prince James appeals against the House of Hanover*
silver medal, 1721

127. *James VIII and III's attempts to recover the throne ridiculed*
silver medal, 1716

129. *The Marriage of 'James VIII' and Clementina*
silver medal, 1719

James's involvement in preparations for a Jacobite rising in 1719 meant that his marriage to Clementina was initially by proxy on 10 May 1719. The medal illustrated (**fig. 129**) probably commemorates that ceremony rather than their actual marriage in September.

Another propaganda message was conveyed on a medal circulated among Jacobites, which depicts the Horse of Hanover trampling the (Stewart) Lion and Unicorn of Britain (**fig. 130**).

Jacobite military strategy in 1719, in alliance with Spain, consisted of an intended landing in the south-west of England and a rising in the Highlands of Scotland. The former attempt was wrecked by a storm,

while the latter resulted in the disastrous battle of Glenshiel, the subject of a painting of 1719 by Peter Tillemans (**fig. 131**).

The battle was fought on the evening of 10 June. The artist's viewpoint is towards the Jacobite positions. Government forces were commanded by General Wightman (on the dark horse in the centre foreground). On the left of the painting Lord George Murray, on the slopes of Sgurr a'Chuilinn, attempts to repulse the initial attack, but he was soon forced to retreat. Hanoverian troops, including two Dutch contingents, then launched an attack on Lord Seaforth's men on Sgurr na Ciste Duibhe on the opposite side of the valley. Despite support from Rob Roy MacGregor, who is probably the figure with

sword and targe, they soon scattered. A decisive attack was then launched in the centre, on the mainly Spanish forces. Collapse quickly followed and the defeated were pursued until dark, up into what is now called the Coirean nan Spainteach.

James and Clementina were married by the Bishop of Montefiascone on the night of 1 September 1719. The painting at the head of this chapter (fig. 120) records the event, which took place in a temporary chapel erected in one of the apartments of his episcopal palace: 'a sacred altar was set up bearing an image of Our Lord Jesus Christ crucified and four candelabra with lighted candles: likewise, a faldstool furnished with silk ... with four cushions for their Royal Majesties'. Among those attending were Mrs John Hay, sister of one of James's most trusted advisers, and Charles Wogan, who had rescued the Princess when she had been detained at Innsbruck on her way to Italy. All of these heads are clearly portraits.

The eighteenth century saw Britain become the leading producer of glass in Europe and its high quality tableware included wine glasses and goblets made both in Scotland and England, with engraved and enamelled emblems, symbols and slogans expressing coded support for the Stewart monarchy in exile. Engraved miniature portraits and

131. *The Battle of Glenshiel, 1719*
oil on canvas, dated 1719
by Peter Tillemans

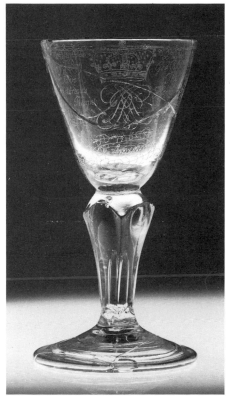

132

133

134

132–4. Jacobite or 'Amen' Glasses

inscriptions alternated with stars, thistles and roses symbolising James VII, his son James Francis Edward, Prince Charles Edward and Prince Henry Benedict. It became a covert fashion around some dinner tables and in shadowy political clubs to toast the exiled Stewarts.

Three examples of glasses used for these toasts are illustrated. The first (**fig. 132**) is a glass engraved with a disguised monogram of 'James VIII', flanked by a Jacobite version of the National Anthem. This was owned by the Murray Thriepland family who had been active supporters of the exiled Stewarts in the Jacobite Risings. The second (**fig. 133**) is a wine glass with characteristic trumpet-shaped

bowl, engraved with the monogram 'JR8' (James VIII) and the Jacobite National Anthem with the concluding 'AMEN' which gives these glasses their name. The third Amen glass (**fig. 134**) is diamond-point engraved with the inscription 'Prosperity to the Bank of Scotland' and 'A Bumper to the Memory of Mr David Drummond, 1743'. Drummond, Treasurer of the Bank, was a staunch Stewart supporter and acted as custodian of the funds raised for the defence of Jacobite prisoners after the 1715 Rising.

135. *Prince Charles Edward*
oil on canvas, dated 1732
by Antonio David

Charles Edward Stewart
('Bonnie Prince Charlie',
'The Young Pretender', 'Charles III')
1720–88

'BONNIE PRINCE CHARLIE' was born in the Muti Palace in Rome amidst great rejoicing. From his earliest days he was spoiled by his adoring household and Jacobites throughout Britain sent anxiously for reports of his progress. His parents quarrelled constantly and his upbringing was left largely in the hands of his tutors, the Scottish Earl of Dunbar and the Irish Sir Thomas Sheridan. Entranced by Sir Thomas's tales of medieval chivalry, he resolved that as soon as he grew up he would win back his father's throne.

In 1744 it seemed that his moment had come. France was going to send an invading force to Britain, led by 'the Young Pretender', as the Hanoverians called him. When this scheme fell through, the Prince was bitterly disappointed, but he was determined to go ahead whether or not he had any assistance. Setting out for Scotland with only a handful of companions, he landed on the island of Eriskay in the Outer Hebrides on 22 July 1745.

He had been relying on the Highland chiefs for support, but now he discovered that they thought his plans rash and foolhardy. By sheer force of personality he gradually won them over, assembled an army and marched to Edinburgh virtually unopposed. Thanks to the skill of his Lieutenant-General, Lord George Murray, he gained a notable victory against the government forces at Prestonpans, and decided to march on London.

The Highland chiefs and Lord George were reluctant, and by the time they reached Derby they were convinced that the expedition could never succeed: George II had not just one army ready but three. The Prince's army refused to go any further and, much against his will, he was forced to retreat. They reached Scotland safely, won a victory at Falkirk but were finally crushed at Culloden.

After months of being hunted through the Western Highlands, Charles escaped to France, to spend the rest of his life in exile, sinking ever deeper into depression and alcoholism. His late marriage to the German Louise of Stolberg was childless and although he styled himself Charles III all hope of a Jacobite restoration had gone. After some years spent in Florence, he returned to the Muti Palace in Rome, where he died in 1788.

136. *The Baptism of Prince Charles Edward*
oil on canvas; by Agostino Masucci and Pier Leone Ghezzi

Many portraits of the young Prince and his brother Henry were painted, virtually from birth, by Antonio David, effectively court painter to the exiled Jacobites from 1718. David was Venetian but worked mainly in Rome. The Princes' father considered David's portraits 'very like'. The prettiness of the portrait of Charles (**fig. 135**) has made it one of the best known Jacobite images. The eleven-year-old Prince wears the star of the Order of the Garter on his left breast, partly covered by the broad blue riband of the Order. Inside his coat is suspended the Thistle badge of St Andrew. His long, auburn hair can be seen under an elegant powdered wig.

When Charles was born in the early evening of 31 December 1720, he was immediately entrusted to his governess, Lady Misset, and within the hour he was baptised by the Bishop of Montefiascone in his mother's chapel in the Muti Palace. He was given the names Charles Edward Louis John Casimir Silvester Xavier Maria. The painting of this event (**fig. 136**), and its companion showing his parents' marriage (**fig. 120**), were painted for the Prince's father a number of years after the events, using engravings and other portraits for the heads. This, and the involvement of a second painter in the depiction of the baptism, must explain the discrepancy in the relative age of James, who is shown looking much older in the marriage scene.

137. *Prince Charles*
bronze medal by Otto Hammerani, about 1729

138. *The Silver-gilt Travelling Canteen of Prince Charles Edward Stewart*
by Ebenezer Oliphant, Edinburgh, 1740–41

139. *Amen glass inscribed 'A Bumper to the Prosperity of the Family of Lochiel'*

A medal by Otto Hammerani (**fig. 137**) represents the young Princes Charles and Henry as second and third in line to the triple throne of Britain. Hammerani was one of the engravers to the papal court and the medal is a very fine example of his work.

Prince Charles's travelling canteen (**fig. 138**), with its cutlery and wine beakers, may have been a twenty-first birthday present from one of his Scottish supporters. The outer case and beakers were made by Ebenezer Oliphant, a member of the staunchly Jacobite family of Oliphant of Gask. The canteen was lost along with much of the Prince's other baggage at the battle of Culloden and fell into the

140. *Weapons of the clansmen*

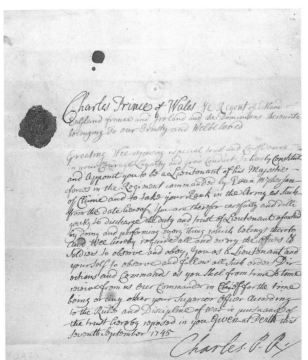

141. *Commission for an officer in the Jacobite Army* 1745

---

hands of the Hanoverian commander, William, Duke of Cumberland. He presented it to his *aide-de-camp* George Keppel, Lord Bury, later Earl of Albemarle. It remained in his family until 1963.

The support of the Camerons of Locheil was regarded by Prince Charles Edward as crucial to the success of the Rising when he arrived on the west coast in 1745. Locheil's role in the campaign is acknowledged on an Amen glass dedicated to the prosperity of his family (**fig. 139**).

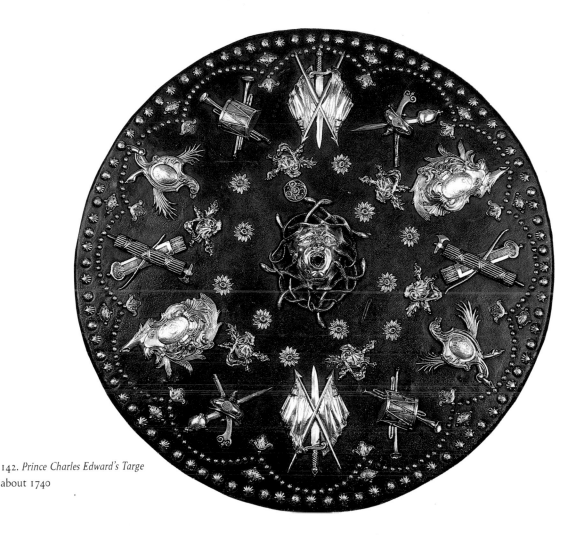

142. *Prince Charles Edward's Targe*
about 1740

In the 1640s the Earl of Montrose, followed by Viscount Dundee in 1689, had raised Highland armies in support of the House of Stewart. These armies, equipped with targes and basket-hilted swords, made short work of the regular forces sent against them, literally charging their opponents in a tactic known as the *dol sios*. Despite poor leadership this manoeuvre again met with success when used by the Jacobite army at Sheriffmuir in 1715. It is not surprising, therefore, that the leaders of the '45 consciously created a tartan army using traditional weapons and tactics.

The targe illustrated (**fig. 140**) is thought to have been carried by the Marquis of Huntly at Sheriffmuir; the dirk is a good example of

the daggers carried by the Highlanders. Both the sword and the pistol were taken at Culloden.

The Prince's army was an organised regimental force, with many of the regiments commanded by clan chiefs and raised from their clansmen and followers. One of these was Ewan Macpherson, younger of Cluny, who raised his clan in Badenoch, aided by a number of blank commissions for officers in his regiment. The commission illustrated (**fig. 141**) is for a lieutenant in 'his Majesties forces', commanded on James VIII's behalf by 'Charles, Prince of Wales etc, Regent of Scotland, England, France and Ireland ...'. The

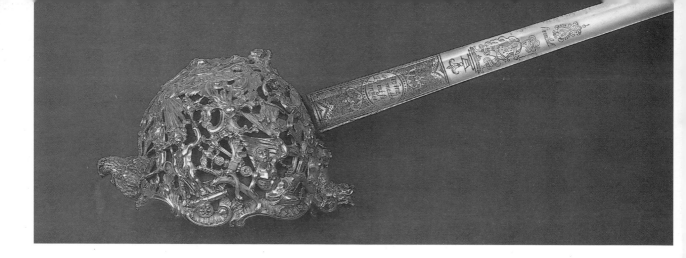

document's seal shows the royal arms quartered for England and France, surrounded by the collar of the Order of the Thistle.

Prince Charles Edward's wooden targe (**fig. 142**) is of typical Highland construction, covered with pigskin but with silver mounts added in London. Made about 1740, it was part of the accoutrements of a complete set of Highland clothes presented to the Prince in 1740 by James, 3rd Duke of Perth. Left behind in a baggage wagon after the defeat at Culloden, it was rescued by Ewan Macpherson of Cluny, a colonel in the Jacobite army. It remained in the possession of the Macphersons of Cluny until this century.

A basket hilted backsword (**fig. 143**) was another part of the accoutrements presented to the Prince by the 3rd Duke of Perth. The Duke commissioned it in London, where the cast silver hilt was made in 1740 by a silversmith called Charles Frederick Kandler. Although very elaborate, the Prince's sword and targe were examples of the typical weapons used by clansmen in his army. Like the targe, the sword was lost at Culloden, and it seems to have come into the possession of the Duke of Cumberland. It certainly remained in the royal collections until 1820, when George IV presented it to MacDonald of Clanranald.

143. *Prince Charles Edward's basket hilted backsword*
1740

144. *Prince Charles Edward's silver knife, fork and spoon*
1737–40

145. *Jacobite Fan*
about 1745

During the Prince's 'wanderings' in the Highlands and Islands after Culloden, MacDonald of Clanranald presented him with a silver knife, fork and spoon on 15 May 1746 (**fig. 144**), along with food and clothing. They were made in Paris, between 1737 and 1740, and were probably bought there by Ranald MacDonald, son of Clanranald. Charles kept them for about six weeks, until he gave them to Dr Murdoch MacLeod as a memento, in gratitude for help with his escape. Engraved with the legend '*ex dono*/CPR [Charles, Prince Regent] /July 3/1746', they remained until recently in the possession of Dr MacLeod's descendants.

After his victory at Prestonpans, Prince Charles gave a ball at Holyroodhouse in Edinburgh at which the ladies were presented with fans. The fan illustrated (**fig. 145**) may be one of these. Made of paper and mounted on ivory, the fan depicts Prince Charles Edward surrounded by classical gods. The figures to the right are reputed to be the family of King George II retreating in confusion. The design is by tradition attributed to Robert Strange, the Jacobite engraver.

The original clay model by Jean-Baptiste Lemoyne for the bronze bust of the Prince (**fig. 146**) was considered to be perhaps the best likeness yet. The model is no longer known but must have been made

146. *Prince Charles Edward Stewart*
bronze bust, after a plaster replica, dated 1746
by Jean-Baptiste Lemoyne

147. *Touchpieces*
about 1603–1788

shortly after the 1745 uprising, when Charles arrived back in Paris to a hero's welcome in spite of his defeat. The sculptor received a total of 8000 *livres* in April and May 1747 for various busts of him. This one was to be the study for a marble bust, but its form is now known only in a number of later plaster casts.

The ancient belief that the monarch could cure the disease scrofula ('The King's Evil') by touching the sufferer gave rise to the giving of tokens or touchpieces (**fig. 147**). James VI and his successors made use of the custom to promote belief in the Divine Right of the monarchy. Originally a gold coin, an 'angel' was given to those who

had been 'touched'. As this ceremony became more popular – Charles I was said to have touched ninety thousand people during his reign – silver medalets were introduced instead, to reduce the cost.

The last ruling British monarch to perform the ceremony was Queen Anne. It was rejected by the Protestant Hanoverians, but was continued by the Stewarts in exile, who used it to bolster their claim to a God-given right to the throne.

The 'four peers' ring (**fig. 148**) commemorates the four Jacobite Lords executed in 1746–7 for their part in the Rising: Kilmarnock, Derwentwater, Balmerino and Lovat. A family tradition says that

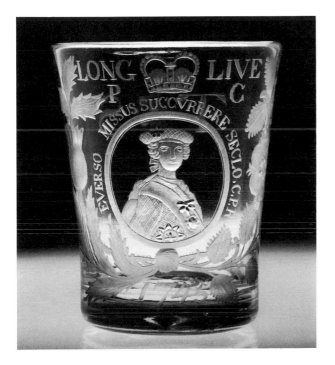

such rings were made by Ebenezer Oliphant, the Edinburgh goldsmith who made Prince Charles's silver canteen.

The bust by J.-B. Lemoyne (**fig. 146**) was probably the source for the image of Charles that appears on a gold medallion of about 1750. Two examples of the medallion are illustrated (**fig. 149**), one set in a ring. The hoop of the ring is inscribed 'CPR' (Charles, Prince Regent) and 'DUM SPIRAT SPERO' ('While he lives, I hope'). The medallions were probably struck in Paris by Adam Tait, an exiled Edinburgh goldsmith who had fled to France after the '45.

A late eighteenth-century glass (**fig. 150**) features Robert Strange's portrait of the Prince, though as the picture is reversed the Garter sash appears on the wrong shoulder. The Latin motto, 'Sent to support a fallen age', had appeared on a medal of 1661 struck for the coronation of Charles II. The engraved '1745' is commemorative.

A silver medal of 1750 (**fig. 151**) represents Prince Charles as a flourishing sapling of the oak tree which symbolises the House of Stewart. The medal was issued by a Jacobite society in London to keep the cause alive.

152. *Prince Charles Edward Stewart*
oil on canvas
by Hugh Douglas Hamilton

153. *Charlotte, Duchess of Albany (1753–89)*
oil on canvas
by Hugh Douglas Hamilton

154. *Wine glass with enamelled portrait
of Prince Charles Edward*
about 1775

By the time the Prince's portrait was painted by Hugh Douglas Hamilton in 1785 (**fig. 152**) both his appearance and his character had deteriorated. A contemporary described him as 'irritable, morose and intractable, particularly in his family', owing, it seemed to 'an unhappy propensity to wine'. The elderly 'Young Pretender' wears the blue riband of the Garter, the star just visible on his breast. His own short hair is tied with a black bow beneath his wig.

Charlotte, Duchess of Albany (**fig. 153**), was the illegitimate daughter of Prince Charles and his Scottish mistress, Clementina Walkinshaw, who lived with him in the Low Countries. Mother and daughter eventually fled from his increasing violence, but he and Charlotte were reconciled in 1784 and she cared for him in his final years. He bestowed on her the title of Duchess of Albany (not to be confused with his wife, Louise of Stolberg, who bore the title Countess of Albany). A contemporary commented that Charlotte could not be called handsome, because 'the features of her face resemble too much those of her father', but she was judged 'gay, lively, very affable and has the behaviour of a well-bred Frenchwoman'. Her reconciliation with Charles seems to have resulted in a number of portraits in both pastels and oils by the Irish artist Hamilton, who was active in Florence and Rome.

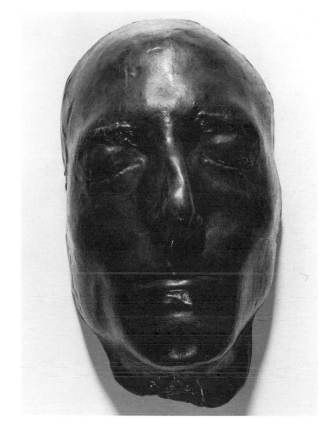

155. *Death-mask of Prince Charles Edward* electrotype of a plaster mask

A rare portrait glass (**fig. 154**) was one of a set of six commissioned about 1775 by Thomas Erskine, later 9th Earl of Kellie. Erskine was a member of a group of aristocratic Jacobites who met annually for dinner in the home of the Edinburgh lawyer James Steuart, to celebrate the birthday of Prince Charles Edward. This glass is said to have been last used at the final such dinner on 31 December 1787, a few weeks before the Prince's death.

On the death of Prince Charles in 1788 a plaster death mask was taken which has now disappeared. The traditional belief is that it was made by a member of a Roman family of modellers called Lucchesi. It

has also been associated with Canova's relief portrait of Charles on the Stewart monument in St Peter's. In 1839 the mask was brought by Bernardino Lucchesi to Glasgow and used by a number of sculptors, including William Mossman. At this time it was said still to bear hairs from the Prince's eyebrows and eyelashes. These hairs were later removed and the mask painted. An electrotype (**fig. 155**) was made shortly afterwards.

156. *Prince Henry Benedict Stewart*
oil on canvas, dated 1732
by Antonio David

Henry Benedict, Cardinal York
('Henry IX')
1725–1807

157. *Book binding of Prince Henry Benedict, Cardinal York*

JAMES Francis Edward's younger son Henry was also his favourite, a quiet, intellectual, devout boy much more like himself in character than the impetuous Charles. Too young to accompany the Prince on his mission in 1745, Henry greeted his brother gladly on his return and took him to his lodgings in Paris. It was not long, however, before they were quarrelling violently over Charles's heavy drinking and one night Henry slipped away and rode for Rome. He had decided to become a priest, and indeed before long he was made a Cardinal.

Charles was furious. Always aware that the Protestant British disapproved of the Jacobite Stewarts' religion, he and his father had tried not to emphasise their allegiance to the Roman Catholic Church. Now Henry had drawn attention to it in the most noticeable way possible, and Charles felt betrayed. He forbade Henry's name to be mentioned in his presence, and declared that he would never see their father again, since he had condoned the decision.

Henry meanwhile pursued a successful ecclesiastical career, becoming Archbishop of Corinth in 1759 and Bishop of Tusculum in 1761. He built up a fine library at his palace at Frascati, and tried to encourage a reconciliation with Charles. The Prince steadfastly refused to return as long as their father was alive, but when he did finally move south to Italy Henry welcomed him, tried to persuade him to stop drinking, consoled him when his wife ran away with her Italian lover and gave him financial support.

When Charles eventually died, he styled himself 'Henry IX', but it was an empty title. He lost most of his money during the French Revolution and his palace was sacked by the French army. The British government arranged his escape to Venice and George III sent him money. Eventually he was able to go back to Frascati and there he died, leaving the few British crown jewels still in his possession and the Stewart papers to the Prince Regent. He was buried in St Peter's in Rome, with Charles and their father. Above them is a handsome marble monument by Canova, commissioned by the Prince Regent, the future George IV of Great Britain.

The portrait of Henry by Antonio David (fig. 156) is the companion to the painting by the same artist of Henry's elder brother (fig. 135). They seem to have been painted for the Jacobite soldier of fortune, Charles Wogan. A letter from James Francis Edward to Wogan in January 1732 probably refers to them: 'My children's pictures are doing for you, so that you will soon have them'. Henry, like his brother, is shown with the badge and riband of the Garter. The painter has indulged himself in the splendours of the silver cuff and the waves of natural hair that fall from under the child's wig.

Prince Henry Benedict's coat of arms, made up with different stamps and surmounted by a Cardinal's hat are embossed on the red leather book binding illustrated (fig. 157). All surviving examples of his arms have the 'cadency mark' of a crescent in the centre, showing that he was a second son.

On the death of Prince Charles Edward, Henry, Cardinal York, inherited the Stewart claim to the throne. A bronze medal of 1788 (fig. 158) draws attention to his right to be 'Henry IX'.

158. *Prince Henry Benedict, Cardinal York's claim to the throne*
bronze medal, 1788

159. *Prince Henry Benedict, Cardinal York*
oil on canvas
by an unknown artist

Although he styled himself 'Henry IX' after his brother's death, Henry made no claim to the throne, recognising that by then all hopes of a Jacobite restoration had finally faded away. The original of the painting illustrated (**fig. 159**) was a three-quarter length portrait by the Roman artist Domenico Corvi which must have been painted shortly after Henry was made Cardinal York in 1747. The portrait shown is one of a number of reduced versions.

160. *Queen Elizabeth,*
Queen of the United Kingdom
of Great Britain and Northern
Ireland (born 1926)
oil on canvas
by Sir William Hutchison

THIS study from life of Queen Elizabeth was painted in 1956 in preparation for a full-length portrait in which Her Majesty is shown wearing the robes of the Order of the Thistle.

Although the Jacobite Stewart line ended with Prince Henry Benedict, many descendants of the Stewart monarchs are alive today, scattered throughout the world. Most notably, Her Majesty The Queen, through her ancestor Sophia of Hanover, is the direct descendant of James VI, Mary, Queen of Scots, the early Stewart monarchs and King Robert the Bruce.